MW00912712

OUTWARD BOUND
CANOEING HANDBOOK

Also available
Outward Bound First Aid Handbook
Outward Bound Map and Compass Handbook
Outward Bound Walker's Handbook

OUTWARD BOUND
CANOEING HANDBOOK

Maggie Annat

WARD LOCK

I would like to thank Des George,
David Evans and Kathy, Hugo
and Jack Iffla for all their support.

The publisher would like to thank
Outward Bound, Aberdovey for their help.

A WARD LOCK BOOK
First published in the UK in 1995
by Ward Lock
Villiers House
41/47 Strand
London WC2N 5JE

A Cassell Imprint

Copyright © Ward Lock 1995

All rights reserved. No part of this publication may be reproduced in any material form (including
photocopying or storing it in any medium by electronic means and whether or not transiently or
incidentally to some other use of this publication) without the written permission of the
copyright owner, except in accordance with the provisions of the Copyright, Designs and Patents
Act 1988 or under the terms of a licence issued by the Copyright Licensing Agency, 90
Tottenham Court Road, London W1P 9HE. Applications for the copyright owner's written
permission to reproduce any part of this publication should be addressed to the publisher.

Outward Bound is a registered trade mark of the Outward Bound Trust Limited as is its device.
The Outward Bound Human Resources Limited (Registration number 2876300). Registered
Office: Chestnut Field, Regent Place, Rugby CV21 2PJ, England.

Distributed in Australia by
Capricorn Link (Australia) Pty Ltd
2/13 Carrington Road, Castle Hill, NSW 2154

British Library Cataloguing-in-Publications data
A catalogue record for this book is available from the British Library

ISBN 0-7063-7308-1

Line illustrations: Tony Randell and Ben Cracknell
Front cover photograph: Stephen Whitehorne
Back cover photograph: Mark Allen Publishing

Typesetting and design: Ben Cracknell
Printed and bound in Finland by Werner Söderström Oy

Contents

About Outward Bound®

The Outward Bound Trust provides high-quality courses in a range of exciting outdoor activities. Our fully qualified instructors maintain the highest standards of tuition, and our safety record is second to none. Everyone who takes an Outward Bound course enjoys a rewarding and memorable experience, the benefits of which will last a lifetime.

Outward Bound courses have been available in Britain since 1941. The original courses were the outcome of a meeting between Kurt Hahn, the educator, and Lawrence Holt, the owner of a shipping line. The marriage of the worlds of education and business is a vital feature of the Outward Bound movement. The courses are both a valuable adjunct to formal education and an important part of career development.

From its beginnings in Britain the Outward Bound movement has spread throughout the world, with 38 centres in 23 countries.

A typical course in the UK lasts from one to three weeks and may be based at one of our five national centres or may take the form of an expeditionary journey by foot or by sailing boat in a wilderness setting. We run courses for all age groups, from 14 to 70!

The Outward Bound Trust also works directly with industry in designing programmes to help companies through periods of change. This may involve developing leadership skills for young managers or assisting in building cohesive teams. The courses balance challenging outdoor tasks with reflection and review. They are specially designed so that participants can always translate what they gain from a course back to their working environment.

After an Outward Bound experience, people discover many positive attributes about themselves. They become more confident; they learn to share; to lead and to follow; to understand their own strengths and to work together as a group. By safeguarding each other, they form bonds of trust. They discover that many problems can be solved only with the co-operation of all members of a group.

To find out more about Outward Bound courses or to request a brochure, please contact us at the address below:

Outward Bound Trust
Head Office
Chestnut Field
Regent Place
Rugby CV21 2PJ

Tel (0788) 560423

Ian Fothergill
Director, Outward Bound Trust

1

Introduction

History

Nearly all over the world the canoe is recognized as the world's oldest, most traditional form of boat used for hunting, transport and travel. The shape and design of canoes has varied widely in different regions of the world depending on the materials available and the canoe's usage.

As far as terminology goes there are two basic types of canoe – the *kayak*, which is descended from the boats used by coastal Eskimos, and the *canoe* made of birchbark, built by North American Indians for use on inland rivers and lakes.

In this book the term 'canoe' will be used to refer to both types of craft (kayak and canoe) and where it is necessary to distinguish between the two they will be referred to as 'kayak' and 'open canoe'.

I will briefly mention four kinds of canoe here that contrast a little with each other, but there are many variations all over the world, both in design and materials, some of which are still in use today and others which, sadly, are a dying tradition.

The *dugout* is typical of tropical forest regions. It is a very primitive canoe made from logs which are hollowed by burning or cutting away the inside of the log.

The *birchbark canoe* of North America (probably the most famous of canoes) was built with bark from birch trees stitched firmly over a light frame of wooden ribs. This type of canoe has virtually disappeared, but was significant in the early exploration of northern parts of North America where tree growth was so dense, that travel by rivers and lakes was by far the easiest method of getting around.

The *quajaq*, pronounced 'kayak', of the Inuit and its bigger, slower counterpart the *umiak* were both made of sealskin or walrus skin. The skin was chewed to make it supple before being stretched and tightened over a frame of bone and driftwood. The frame was held together with thong lacing and ties, which were sometimes made out of the rear flipper of a ring seal. The skin was stitched in place using the leg sinews of caribou. The kayak, being used at sea, needed to keep waves out so there was only a small hole, called the cockpit, where the kayaker sat. Covering the gap that was left was a sealskin spray cover. The kayak, which was long and narrow in the water, used a double-bladed paddle and was paddled by hunters who were traditionally men. The large, spacious umiak was capable of carrying several people and was paddled by the women.

The long *war canoes* built by islanders in the Pacific Ocean were heavier canoes. They were built with outriggers, which are frameworks projecting from the side of the canoe to a float, to act as stabilizers. These canoes needed many people to power them through the huge waves and surf that pounded the coral reefs.

The European canoe

In 1865 John MacGregor, a Scottish barrister, designed the *Rob Roy*, which was the first European canoe derived from the canoes John MacGregor had seen in North America and northern Russia. The *Rob Roy* was of a kayak variety, but shorter and wider than the Inuit kayak. It was made of wood and included a space for a mast and sail.

The growth of canoeing as a sport was mainly due to the formation of the Royal Canoe Club, which held races attracting more people to the sport and then later, to the development of a folding canvas canoe, the *Klepper*, which was brought out just before the First World War. In the late 1920s came the rediscovery of rolling (which the Inuits already practised), the art of righting the kayak after a capsize, which gave paddlers greater versatility in the use of their craft.

Canoe clubs

The best way of getting started is with suitably qualified or experienced people where learning will be quicker and more fun. Canoe clubs are generally established in major towns all over the country, and although they may not always be able to offer you exactly what you want, they will certainly be good sources for information and contacts, including the selling of second-hand boats.

A club's activities will generally be determined by the kind of water easily accessible to it. Some clubs may specialize in only one or two canoeing disciplines and it really is a diverse sport so do not be put off if you cannot find what you want immediately.

Canoe courses

There are multitudes of people and places that offer canoe courses – for the beginner, intermediate or advanced canoeist; on placid water such as lakes, or on rivers, estuaries and the sea. Some people prefer to go on a course as a taster before committing themselves to buying a canoe while others prefer to buy one first and then go out and learn. It is important for you to make sure that you will be in the care of suitably qualified and experienced canoeists when you apply for a course.

The British Canoe Union

The British Canoe Union (BCU) is the national governing body for all aspects of canoeing within the UK. It represents the interests of canoeists at local, national and international levels and is a member of the International Canoe Federation (ICF). The BCU consists of federal associations representing Wales, Scotland and Northern Ireland, divided further into regions which have local voluntary officers, including a Regional Coaching Organizer and several Local Coaching Organizers.

The BCU has a coaching service which trains and qualifies instructors and coaches at all levels and branches of the sport. It also has a comprehensive system of tests and awards for personal performance as well as qualifications for those wishing to coach or teach canoeing.

Membership of the BCU is open to all who are interested in canoeing. The National Associations can give you information on clubs in your area, people with similar interests to your own and lists of approved centres and organizations running courses.

See pages 194-5 for the addresses of National Associations in the UK, and contact addresses in other countries.

2

Canoes and equipment

You can appreciate that with such a diverse sport as canoeing there are many different types of canoe and equipment. Almost every year styles and designs change to make faster, more manoeuvrable craft. Not everything can be covered in this book, but what will be covered is canoeing equipment for beginners with information on what to do and where to go next.

Types of canoes

There is not really one canoe that performs everything perfectly. There always has to be a compromise – competition versus recreation, or flat water versus rivers or sea. For example, long, thin canoes, although less stable, will go faster than short, wide canoes, which are more stable. So stability and speed are not really compatible. There are general purpose canoes which are good for the beginner and more specialist boats available for those with more familiarity with the sport.

Construction

Knowledge of materials and construction is constantly progressing. The choice of material has a lot to do with canoe usage, strength, weight, durability and design. Glass-reinforced plastic (more commonly known as fibreglass) appeared in the 1960s making canoe design possibilities endless. Canoes became cheaper, lighter in weight, stronger and easier to repair. The 1980s saw the creation of the polyethylene canoe which, when deformed, regains its original shape, leaving only a few creases. However, polyethylene is heavier than fibreglass and subject to abrasion when scraped or dragged over rocks and so on.

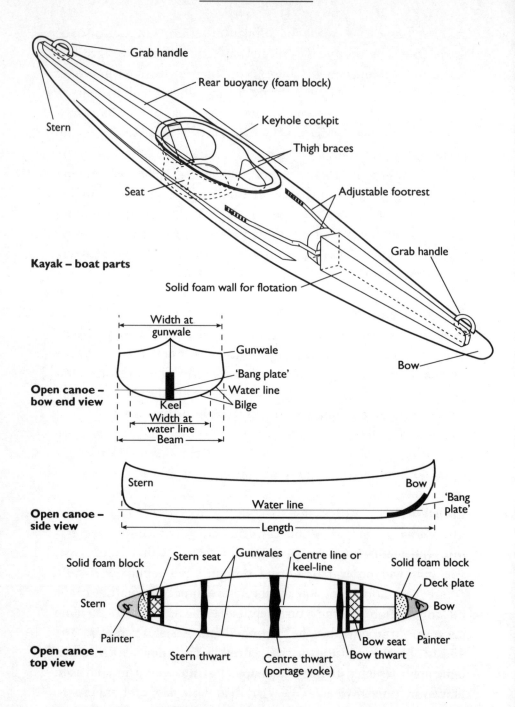

Grab handle

Rear buoyancy (foam block)

Keyhole cockpit

Stern

Thigh braces

Seat

Adjustable footrest

Kayak – boat parts

Grab handle

Solid foam wall for flotation

Bow

Width at gunwale

Gunwale

'Bang plate'

Water line

**Open canoe –
bow end view**

Keel

Bilge

Width at
water line

Beam

Stern

Bow

Water line

'Bang
plate'

**Open canoe –
side view**

Length

Solid foam block

Stern seat

Gunwales

Centre line or
keel-line

Solid foam block

Deck plate

Stern

Bow

Painter

Painter

**Open canoe –
top view**

Stern thwart

Centre thwart
(portage yoke)

Bow seat

Bow thwart

2.1 Identifying parts of the kayak and the open canoe.

Open canoes are made of similar materials, but can also be made from aluminium. Aluminium is virtually maintenance-free and can withstand lots of abuse, but it is cold to sit in in winter and difficult to repair. There are many other combinations or hybrids of materials such as Royalex, Crosslink 3 and ABS (acrylonitrile-butadiene-styrene), which is known by its abbreviation because it is too complex a name to remember. These canoes are also heavy and difficult to repair, but are very durable, require little maintenance and regain their shape when deformed.

Competition canoes are usually made from strong, yet light-weight materials, because the weight as well as the stiffness or rigidity of these canoes is more critical for quick manoeuvring and speed.

Volume

Body weight also affects the type of kayak that you should buy. This is because the volume of kayaks varies and they will only support a person up to a specified weight. Volume is the amount of air that is surrounded by the kayak's shell (the deck and hull combined) and determines the total weight it can float.

Design and stability

A canoe's design affects its stability. Generally, wide canoes are more stable than narrow canoes. Also flatter hulls or shallow V-shaped hulls are more stable than very rounded U-shaped hulls.

Manoeuvrability

The very bottom of the canoe (the keel-line) is curved as well. This is called 'rocker'. Rocker is the amount of curve the canoe has from bow to stern, a bit like a banana. The more rocker then the more manoeuvrable the canoe will be. A lot of rocker is particularly useful in slalom canoes where fast turning is vital, but it is not so useful on the sea or canals where tracking in a straight line is preferred.

Low volume slalom kayak made of fibreglass. This is a competition kayak and good
for small people and children to learn in. It has no space to put equipment
183l (6½ cubic ft) volume: 400cm (158in) long

Medium volume kayak made of polyethylene. The greatest number of kayaks are in
this range. It is suitable for beginners and up to medium grade white water
250l (9 cubic ft) volume: 355cm (139in) long

Higher volume kayak made of polyethylene. This is suitable for beginners and all levels
of white water. It is a play-boat and is much shorter than the others
261l (9.3 cubic feet) volume: 287cm (112in) long

2.2 Different volume in kayaks.

Parts of the canoe and important fittings

Whether you buy a new or second-hand canoe there are a few
things which should be included and need to be checked. The
canoe on its own is not safe enough without these fittings.

Cockpit

In a kayak this is the place where you sit. Many modern kayaks
have a keyhole-shaped cockpit which makes getting out easier in
the event of a capsize. The keyhole cockpit is long enough for an
average-sized person to put their knees together and slide their
legs out while still sitting on the seat, so you do not really have
to use your hands to get out. Other kayaks have smaller cockpits
which take more confidence to get out of in a capsize.

Round-bilged or shallow-arched hull

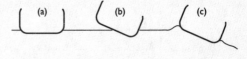

(a) Primary stability. These hulls appear less stable on flat water than flat-bottomed hulls because there is less of the hull in the water. However they offer the best all-round performance

(b) Secondary stability. When the canoe is leaned on flat or moving water the widest part of the hull is in the water, so its stability is greater

(c) On waves the canoe rocks less than the flat-bottomed hull and is therefore easier to keep upright. They perform well in waves and white water

Flat-bottomed hull

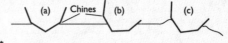

(a) Primary stability. This hull appears very stable on flat water. They are good for general recreation where initial stability is needed

(b) Secondary stability. When the boat is leaned, less hull is in the water making it less stable than when kept level

(c) On waves it rocks from side to side a lot and demands an effort from paddlers to keep it upright in rough water

Shallow V-shaped hull

(a) Primary stability. This hull appears less steady on flat water. Only a small surface area is in contact with the water so initially it will rock from side to side onto its chines and feel less stable

(b) Secondary stability. When leaned its stability is much greater as more hull is placed in the water at its widest part. This design is the most stable overall although it is not as fast in the water as the round-bilged hull

2.3 Hulls in cross-section to show how hull shape affects primary and secondary stability in kayaks and open canoes.

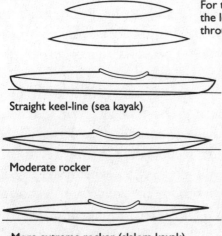

Straight keel-line (sea kayak)

Moderate rocker

More extreme rocker (slalom kayak)

For two canoes with the same width, the longer canoe travels faster through the water

A boat with little rocker will go in a straight line. A boat with a rockered hull will perform like a shorter boat, because not all of its length is in the water – it will turn faster

To select a canoe that performs how you want it to (straight or manoeuvrable), you have to imagine how deep the canoe floats in the water and what shape it will be at its water line

2.4 Speed versus manoeuvrability.

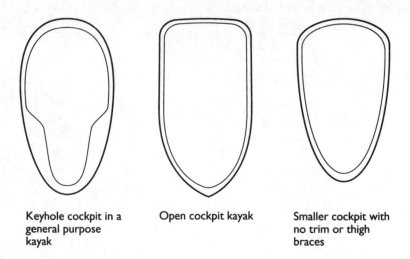

Keyhole cockpit in a
general purpose
kayak

Open cockpit kayak

Smaller cockpit with
no trim or thigh
braces

2.5 Cockpit designs.

Buoyancy

A canoe will sink if it is full of water. To prevent it sinking manufacturers build buoyancy into the canoes when they are new.
Buoyancy is usually in the form of solid foam walls, air bags or a
combination of both and should be placed evenly in both bow
and stern. This should be firmly attached or tied in place so that it
will not be forced out if the canoe becomes full of water. You
cannot have too much buoyancy to be safe.

If you progress to paddling in white water I would strongly
advise that you fill all the available space in the bow and stern
with buoyancy. In an open canoe, if paddling tandem, fill the
centre section as well as smaller sections in the bow and stern.
When paddling solo, fill all but the section where you kneel.
Buoyancy reduces the space which can fill with water and adds
more strength to the shape of the canoe, increasing safety, as
canoes are not as likely to deform in white water if pinned with
any force against obstructions.

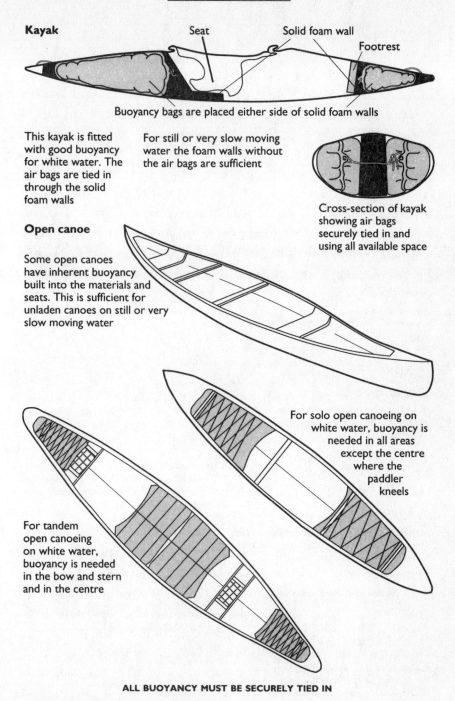

Kayak

Seat

Solid foam wall

Footrest

Buoyancy bags are placed either side of solid foam walls

This kayak is fitted with good buoyancy for white water. The air bags are tied in through the solid foam walls

For still or very slow moving water the foam walls without the air bags are sufficient

Cross-section of kayak showing air bags securely tied in and using all available space

Open canoe

Some open canoes have inherent buoyancy built into the materials and seats. This is sufficient for unladen canoes on still or very slow moving water

For solo open canoeing on white water, buoyancy is needed in all areas except the centre where the paddler kneels

For tandem open canoeing on white water, buoyancy is needed in the bow and stern and in the centre

ALL BUOYANCY MUST BE SECURELY TIED IN

2.6 Buoyancy or flotation in canoes.

Footrests (kayaks only)

A footrest helps you control the kayak when paddling, It enables you to push with your feet and legs, using your whole body not just your arms. It also stops you sliding down the kayak if you hit something at speed or if the angle of the boat changes from the horizontal position, especially in white water or surfing.

The footrest should be adjusted so that the balls of your feet rest against it and your legs are held with your knees apart and in contact with the knee or thigh braces (or underside of the cockpit if you do not have any braces). It is important that the footrest will not trap your feet if they were to go beyond it. This is of particular concern with bar type footrests which should be failsafe and be allowed to pivot, freeing your feet easily if they were to get caught.

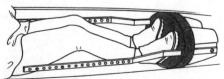

Shock absorbing, full plate footrest
Suitable for any form of kayaking, it is adjusted by moving the alloy bars towards or away from the cockpit

Open cockpit footrest
Not suitable for closed cockpit kayaks. The side pieces are moulded to the kayak. The cross-piece is bolted in place

Serrated or shark's tooth footrest
This provides a limited number of foot places. It is not suitable in white water.

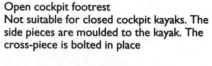

Pedal footrest
The pedals slide up and down on the track. This is all right in easy water

Fail-safe footrest
The alloy bar is held in place by flanges moulded to the kayak. One side of the bar is fixed with a bolt, the other pivots towards the cockpit when moved

2.7 Different types of footrests in kayaks.

Grab handle on a kayak

A good system. It is safe and strong and can easily be clipped for towing or rescue. It does not trap fingers. It is made of rope or rigid plastic, which may be difficult to replace but is strong

Toggle on a kayak

Another good system as long as the rope or webbing to which the toggle attaches is kept in good condition. It is easy to replace. It can also have a ball of rope or other small object instead of a toggle

Rope loop on a kayak

Only suitable for still or very slow moving water. The rope loop will trap fingers if the kayak spins in rough water or waves. Some people tie a short piece of webbing to the loop to grab hold of in white water

Rope loop on an open canoe

Again this is suitable for still or very slow moving water. It is better if the painter and the rope loop are one piece, spliced together

Keep loop as small as possible

Painter spliced or tied with a knot in the bow – used as a grab line and suitable for white water

2.8 Toggles and grab handles.

Toggles and grab handles

A kayak is inherently very slippery so it is important that you or someone else can grab hold of it in the event of it floating away or if you and your kayak need towing or rescuing. The toggles or grab handles must be fitted to both ends of the kayak. They should be strong, provide somewhere easy to clip a towline to and not trap your fingers if the kayak was to spin in the water while you were holding onto it, the latter being especially important in white water.

Decklines

These are lengths of rope, 8mm (¼in) in diameter, secured to the deck of the kayak to extend the principle of the grab handles.

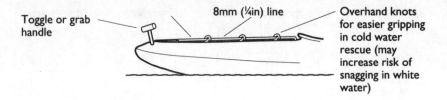

Toggle or grab handle

8mm (¼in) line

Overhand knots for easier gripping in cold water rescue (may increase risk of snagging in white water)

The deckline is secured here through a hole in the deck or a special recessed fitting in front of the cockpit. Make the hole as small as possible and seal it with a piece of neoprene and sealant to prevent leaks. Tie the other end tightly to the original end loop. The decklines need to be adjusted so they are always tight. One deckline is fitted to the bow and the other to the stern

Painter secured correctly to the deck plate on an open canoe. It should not be tied but looped or coiled and placed under elastic on the deck plate

Stow the rope from the end so when it is released it pulls out towards the end of the canoe and does not strain the elastic

Elastic on deck plate

2.9 Decklines and painters fitted to canoes.

However, some white water paddlers choose not to fit them due to their potential for snagging on trees. This can be prevented by ensuring that they are always tight and snug to the deck. They should not however run along the edge of the cockpit, as this could tangle with you and become a hazard. There should be two separate pieces of rope, one secured to each deck.

Painters

Open canoes should have painters. These are two lengths of rope made of a buoyant material such as polypropylene. For non-moving water these only need to be 1–2m (3–6 ft) long, but for white water they should be 4–5m (13–15 ft) long. One painter should be attached to each end of the open canoe through the hull itself, which is the strongest part of the boat. They are used as extensions of the grab handle principle.

Painters are also useful as lines with which to secure the boat on the shore so it does not float away, for tying it onto a roof rack, or for ease in handling down slippery banks. If you paddle on white water then the painter must not have knots or anything else left tied in it as these will be hazardous and snag and get caught on obstructions such as trees and rocks.

Painters should be attached and stowed on the canoe as shown in the diagram. They should not be tied up but looped or coiled and secured under a piece of elastic attached to the deck plate. The painter is then easily pulled free by grabbing hold of it.

Other equipment

The following equipment is much more personal to the paddler and so it is important that you get what is right for you. The right size, fit and comfort are determined by what you want to do and your body's shape and size. If you buy things that do not fit you well you probably will not wear them and then you will not be as safe as you should be.

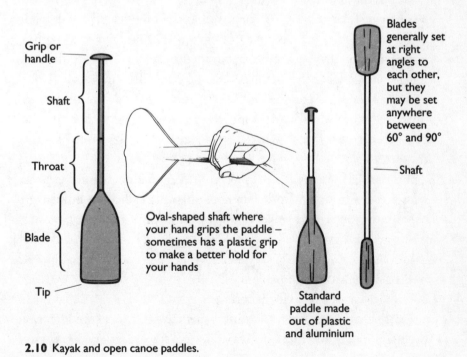

Grip or handle

Shaft

Throat

Blade

Tip

Oval-shaped shaft where your hand grips the paddle – sometimes has a plastic grip to make a better hold for your hands

Standard paddle made out of plastic and aluminium

Blades generally set at right angles to each other, but they may be set anywhere between 60° and 90°

Shaft

2.10 Kayak and open canoe paddles.

Paddles

The type of paddle you choose will depend on your canoe. Paddles are as wide in variety as the canoes. The kayak paddle consists of the shaft or loom and two blades – one at each end set at right angles to each other. This angle is usually between 80 degrees and 90 degrees, but until you do a lot of paddling, the exact figure is not critical.

The open canoe paddle has a single blade, a shaft and a handle or grip.

Kayak paddle

To determine an approximate length of paddle for you, stand the paddle upright, next to you, with one blade on the ground. If you can reach up to the other and curl your fingers over the top of it with your elbow still slightly bent, this should be a reasonable length for you, until you decide that you want to specialize in a particular aspect of the sport. The maximum length of paddle for a person about 1.8m (6ft) tall for sea kayaking would be no more than 2.2m (7ft 2in) long and for white water, no longer than 2.04m (6ft 7in). As a beginner you will be better off with a shorter paddle than a longer one and the shorter the paddle you can get away with the better. I am 1.72m (5ft 8in) tall and use 2.10m (6ft 8in) paddles on both the sea and white water. Although these are a little long for me on white water, it is a reasonable compromise which allows me to use the same paddle for both.

The shaft of the paddle can be round or flattened into an oval where your hands will be. The oval shape is a distinct advantage in helping you to know what the blade is doing without always having to look at it.

The cost of a paddle

The cost of a paddle will depend on what material it is made of. Plastic blades with alloy shafts are the cheapest, but some more expensive types are more robust. The blades are generally flat or curved if made of plastic and curved or asymmetric if made from anything else.

Types of blade

Flat blades can be used for left- or right-handed paddling, but curved and asymmetric blades are either right- or left-handed. The flat and curved paddles are good general purpose blades, whereas asymmetrics are more specialized, being used for touring or flat water racing. If you become a keen paddler then you will quickly progress to curved blades as they grip the water better. Split paddles are ones that come in two halves with a join in the centre of the shaft and are usually carried as spares. They can be curved or flat and set up as both right- or left-handed.

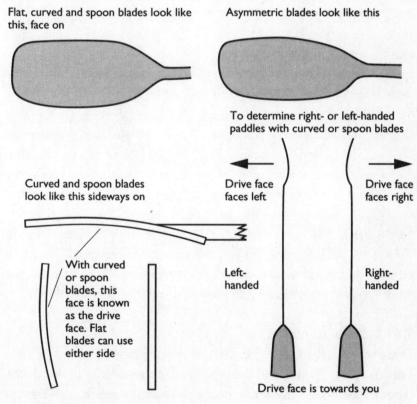

Flat, curved and spoon blades look like this, face on

Asymmetric blades look like this

To determine right- or left-handed paddles with curved or spoon blades

Curved and spoon blades look like this sideways on

Drive face faces left

Drive face faces right

With curved or spoon blades, this face is known as the drive face. Flat blades can use either side

Left-handed

Right-handed

Drive face is towards you

2.11 Types of blade shape.

Right-handed or left-handed paddles?

When buying paddles that are fixed right- or left-handed you do need to know which hand will be your preferred *fixed* hand or *control* hand and it does not necessarily have to do with whether you are right- or left-handed. I am right-handed but prefer to paddle left-handed and it took me a while to work this out when I first started to canoe. For some reason I was unable to paddle in a straight line when paddling right-handed, but as soon as I changed to left-handed I had no problem. So I would advise practising first (maybe change hands) until you are certain which you prefer.

To tell if a paddle is right- or left-handed, stand one blade on the ground in front of you with the curve, the drive face, facing you. Whichever direction the drive face on the upper blade now faces, determines if it is a right- or left-handed paddle.

Open canoe paddles

Again for the correct length stand the paddle upright on the ground in front of you; the top of the handle should come between your chin and forehead. The cost of your paddle will likewise depend on the materials. These are constantly changing. Paddles are generally cheaper if made of plastic and alloy, but fibreglass, carbon fibre and all wood are much nicer to paddle with. Bent-shafted paddles are designed more for flat water racing.

The surface of open canoe paddle blades is more than likely to be flat. Generally they do not have curved surfaces like kayak paddles, but there is a wide range of different shaped blades for more specialized types of paddling.

Spray-decks (kayaks)

These fit tightly round the cockpit and require practice beforehand on how to release them so you know what to do in the event of a capsize. They keep water out and warmth in. The size of the kayak cockpit varies greatly and a snug fit is important.

Spray-decks should have a release strap sewn onto the front, attached in such a way that when it is pulled, it peels the spray-deck off the cockpit.

Buoyancy aids and life-jackets

Canoeing is a safe sport with very few accidents, however people do drown even on sheltered water. Some of these people would have had a better chance of survival if they had been wearing some form of personal buoyancy. I strongly suggest that no matter what canoe you choose to go out in, you wear a British Canoe Union approved buoyancy aid, a British Standards' Institute life-jacket, or, in Europe, one which conforms to the Communauté Européenne (CE) regulations.

There are many different types of buoyancy aids and life-jackets and the way to determine which is the best kind for you is to

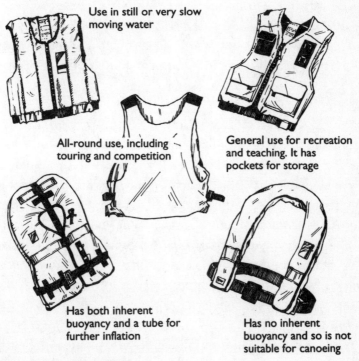

Use in still or very slow moving water

All-round use, including touring and competition

General use for recreation and teaching. It has pockets for storage

Has both inherent buoyancy and a tube for further inflation

Has no inherent buoyancy and so is not suitable for canoeing

2.12 Buoyancy aids and life-jackets.

look at what you will be using it for. For example, a compact, manually inflatable life-jacket suitable for use in offshore sailing boats, is not suitable for canoeing because this type of life-jacket has neither built-in inherent buoyancy nor all round upper body protection which also gives extra thermal insulation. Obtaining personal flotation is not a corner you should cut because it is a vital part of your safety kit.

Buoyancy aid

This is a padded, foam waistcoat that needs to fit snugly over whatever clothing you wear and is secured with an adjustable strap around your waist. The buoyancy aid should not come off accidentally even when it is worn in turbulent water. It should be comfortable to wear, with room for your arms to move freely and should provide a minimum buoyancy of 6kg (13lbs) or be at least 50 newtons (CE specifications).

CE deals in newtons and 1 newton is a measured unit of force, 10 newtons are approximately 1kg (2.2lbs) of buoyancy.

A 50 Newton buoyancy aid = 5kg (11lbs) of buoyancy. And a 100 Newton buoyancy aid = 10.5kg (23lbs) of buoyancy.

Life-jacket

To be classed as a life-jacket the device must conform to British Standards' Institute specifications or one of the two CE life-jacket specifications: 150 newtons (15kg/33lbs) of buoyancy or 275 newtons (28.5 kg/62lbs). The 150 newton life-jacket has equivalent performance to the existing UK approved lifejackets. As a canoeist it is the inherent buoyancy that you should be interested in as well as the potential inflation capabilities. Life-jackets that have both, however, are usually bulky and do not provide all round protection to your upper body as buoyancy aids do.

Helmets

For moving water and surf, helmets are essential. They are not necessary for flat water such as lakes and estuaries. If you buy one

The most common areas for injury are the forehead, temples and nose. These need to be well protected

Poorly fitting helmet: temples and forehead are completely exposed. The helmet cradle is either not adjusted properly or the helmet is too small

Well fitting helmet: the helmet projects forwards enough so that it helps to protect the bridge of the nose

2.13 A helmet that fits correctly is important.

make sure that it fits well and protects your forehead and temples which are where most injuries occur.

Clothing

For the beginner very little specialist clothing is needed. On a sunny, windless day you may get away with shorts, but British weather is not known for its constant sunshine! Canoeing is generally accepted as a wet sport so some form of insulation is important. Wool is a good insulator when wet, but cotton is not. Several thin layers have more insulating properties than one thick layer. Ensure that your trousers will not fall down around your knees and inhibit your swimming ability if you capsize. An old anorak or cagoule will help keep the wind off and should be

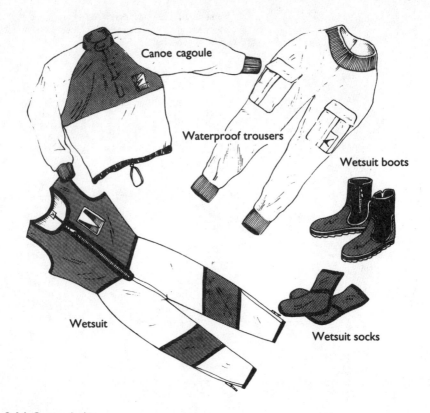

Canoe cagoule

Waterproof trousers

Wetsuit boots

Wetsuit

Wetsuit socks

2.14 Canoe clothing.

worn over the layers of wool. For footwear, well-fitting, lace-up shoes such as old trainers are ideal. Large boots or wellingtons are not suitable as they fill with water and either fall off or are more likely to trap your feet in white water.

As a general guide here are some qualities to look for in old clothing: it needs to have good insulation and retain body warmth when it is wet and it should be quick to dry and comfortable to wear. Wool and most artificial fibres fit into these categories but cotton does not.

For more specialist clothing I would suggest looking in canoeing magazines or wandering around watersports shops to get an idea of the variety available and the cost. If you are interested, then these are the sort of things you could enquire about:

Canoe cagoule

Otherwise known as a 'canoe cag'. This is a windproof layer for the upper body. It needs to have a loose cut around the shoulders to allow for ease of movement and should be as waterproof as possible. A good, durable material is 170g (6oz) weight nylon with neoprene proofing inside.

Wetsuits

These come in a variety of thicknesses, but 3mm (⅛in) is a good thickness for most conditions. It is better to have the sleeveless variety, known as a Long-John, otherwise your arms will be too restricted. Wetsuits only work when they are wet if they are a snug fit. The water they trap between your skin and the neoprene is heated up by your body but you will still need to wear a thin woollen jumper or lightweight, fibre-pile jacket underneath the wetsuit to keep your arms warm. Again two or three thin layers are better than one thick layer.

When do you need to wear a wetsuit? Well there is no exact rule, but if you think you will be swimming a lot or getting soaked by waves and need some extra insulation or protection for your body from scrapes and bruising then it is a good idea to wear a wetsuit. A wetsuit on its own, however, is not windproof and so you will still need to wear a windproof layer over the top.

Wetsuit boots and socks

These are made of neoprene, the same material as the wetsuits. The wetsuit boots have hard soles whereas the wetsuit socks do not, so you need to wear suitable footwear over the socks to give more protection to your feet. Both wetsuit boots and socks are avid collectors of old cheese-like aromas. I have found that rinsing them regularly with soap powder or disinfectant helps keep this under control. This is not very practical on a trip however.

Paddle mitts

These are good in cold or windy weather. They are mitts that fit onto the shaft of the paddle so you can slip your hands into them and still keep in direct contact with the paddle. They can also be lined with an insulating material for extra warmth. I recommend fibre-pile-lined ones for cold conditions. On a four-week river trip I did in the USA (admittedly in winter) the pile-lined paddle mitts were the most sought after objects to' keep our hands warm.

3

Where to canoe

Where can I paddle?

This is probably a question that many people do not think to ask. Many people assume that they can canoe anywhere, but using any stretch of water without permission can be trespassing, which is a civil offence, not a criminal one. The laws in England and Wales, Scotland and Northern Ireland are different. It is not my intention to explain the laws here because they are too involved. I would just like to raise your awareness of this very sensitive topic that is so important in all aspects of outdoor recreation today. More and more people enjoy the outdoor environment and pressure is constantly increasing as people use the world's natural resources for pleasure. Help to make things easier and more pleasant for everybody by showing consideration towards other water users.

Some people find it surprising to believe or difficult to understand, that most of Britain's inland waters and access to them is privately owned. A refusal to accept this fact or ignorance of it, only exacerbates the problem of access. There are people who knowingly or unknowingly gain access to, and paddle, sections of water without enough care and consideration for other people's property or wildlife, and the potential damage they may cause to ongoing and delicate negotiations for access. Contact the British Canoe Union (BCU), Scottish Canoe Association, Welsh Canoe Association, or Canoe Association of Northern Ireland for up-to-date information on access (addresses are on pages 194-5). You will also need to contact the Access Officers for each river you wish to paddle.

Navigation rights

There are places where you are allowed to canoe without obtaining prior permission. These are: ALMOST any stretch of tidal water, the sea, and public and common law navigations.

There is no legal right to navigate along rivers except where a navigational right of way has been established. In most cases the riverside owner owns the bed of the river to the centre line and where a navigation authority is established, all craft have to be registered and/or licensed. Some waterways have easily obtainable licences, and for some rivers the BCU has negotiated access for their members. Other rivers are unmistakably private, and some rivers do have a right of access. There are also many rivers where the navigation rights are in dispute and this is most often where problems occur. There are a few privately owned rivers, where access has been sought and there has been no objection to canoeing at all, and of course the opposite, where cases of not seeking permission have ended up in court. So you can see that the problem is not at all easy to explain, or simple to resolve.

Dealing with and negotiating for access occupies a lot of dedicated time and commitment for people all over the country. The BCU has an Access Committee acting within the law, which deals with problems of access to, or along, sections of water. This is all part of a network of local and regional volunteers, who are keen paddlers, doing their best for canoeists, proving and negotiating with other involved parties and authorities, that canoeists are an environmentally sensitive and concerned group of people.

So before you attempt to take to the water, please spare a thought on behalf of all the parties concerned, and think about where and when you paddle. Do not always believe what you read in guide books as these become rapidly out of date. If you are not sure, or have the slightest doubt about access in your area, contact the following organizations: your regional National Rivers Authority office for information on rivers; British Waterways for information on canals and river navigations under their jurisdiction;or write well in advance, enclosing an S.A.E. for your reply, to the BCU River Information Service in your region. Remember, the BCU is an organization which can be joined for a small annual fee and that these people are there to help with information and advice, NOT to give permission. They are hard working volunteers so please do not make excessive demands of them.

The sea

I will never lose my respect for the sea. The consequences of taking it for granted are serious. I will always remain somewhat daunted by and respectful of this very powerful and changeable force of nature. The sea holds excitement for me because it offers so much diversity. It can be a raging, capricious beast during storms or a vision of tranquil beauty in sunsets. It is unpredictable, with rapidly changing moods and if you are not prepared, be warned. The canoe is quiet, does not pollute and leaves no trace. Seals, sea otters, dolphins, puffins, fulmars and other wildlife become curious or watch, unthreatened, as you drift quietly by at a distance. You can explore cliffs, caves, islands and marshes that no other vessels can see as close. The same trip is never identical, conditions change, you can paddle in waves and exciting tidal races or you can choose smooth and calm, mirror-like seas; and lastly but not least, it does not have to be raining to find enough water.

The sea can be a hostile place for a beginner to learn, unless it is the calmest of weather and water. The weather changes quickly and sometimes what at first was a nice calm day suddenly turns windy, and before you know it the potential for needing outside help becomes very real. Make sure you are with someone who you know is an experienced sea kayaker and will teach you good seamanship.

Access to the sea

Generally access to the sea poses few problems, but in some areas it does, and this will depend on where you would like to go and at what time of the year, as there are some places where access is restricted or controlled. Some sections of coast, and many islands, are coastal reserves and have bird sanctuaries or other wildlife habitations such as seal colonies. Canoeists need to give a wide berth to these protected areas during nesting and nursing seasons. During the breeding season, noise and activity nearby alarms the adults causing them to desert, or permanently abandon, their young. Some birds such as guillemots incubate their eggs on top of their feet, so if they are scared off their nesting site the survival of their eggs or young is put at risk as they are left exposed to predators. Seals will also abandon their pups if they feel threatened and may not return for hours if at all, leaving the pups exposed and vulnerable. Wildlife should not be disturbed by anyone landing on or near these sites or passing too close to them at these important times of the year. If you are in doubt, then keep further away from the cliffs.

In the UK, coastal land that has been established as a Site of Special Scientific Interest (S.S.S.I.) and land owned by the National Trust is subject to particular regulations that must be adhered to.

Surfing beaches

Some of the more popular surfing beaches are divided into sectors for different uses, such as swimmers, surf-boards, canoes and so on, and it is important to abide by the posted regulations for everyone's safety. These beaches are sometimes patrolled by lifeguards, but the same regulations should be practised anywhere where there is a variety of different activities requiring the use of the same water.

There are often conflicts between the various water users occupying the same area and so basic wave etiquette and protocol need to be observed. For example, the first person to ride the wave has the right of way or if two people choose the same wave, the person closest to the shoulder of the wave has right of way. It is sound practice to keep surf-boards and kayaks in different areas if at all possible.

Demarcation zones on beaches

The land on beaches is marked out into different categories. The land below the low water mark (the lowest point that the tide usually reaches) is deemed to be crown land, the land between the low and high water marks is deemed common land and land above the high water mark (the highest point that the tide usually reaches) can be privately owned, so be careful when you try to take your kayak up what looks like a beach.

Firing ranges

Active firing ranges exist along some sections of the coast, which may or may not be marked on the maps. I encountered one such range, which on the map was unmarked, yet behind the beach there was quite an established set-up. However, the ranges usually display a signal when they are firing, such as a series of red flags and sometimes these flags are left up all the time. The coastguard is a good source for information on days and times that firing ranges are active.

Harbours

Depending on where you are, harbours can be busy places for shipping and are usually managed by a Harbour Authority. Shipping has the right of way in restricted waters (under which harbours are classified) and canoeists should keep well clear. Remember that a canoe is a very small craft, unable to be identified as a canoe on a radar and more than likely unable to be distinguished from the blips or clutter, called interference, which is usually associated with waves. Ferries in particular move in and out of harbour walls incredibly quickly and without much warning, and these walls are also great places for fishermen so beware of their lines and hooks.

The coastguard

Her Majesty's Coastguard is responsible for the co-ordination of maritime search and rescue off the coast of the UK. There are 21 locations around the coast that are 24-hour, manned rescue centres called Maritime Rescue Co-ordination Centres (M.R.C.C.) or Maritime Rescue Sub Centres (M.R.S.C.). Both are responsible for the response to incidents within their area. These areas are known as districts. All distress radio calls on VHF channel 16 and the relevant 999 telephone calls are channelled into one of these 21 district headquarters.

Lifeboats and search and rescue (S.A.R.) helicopters carry out the majority of the coastguard's responses to incidents on the sea. Radio communications are essential to the coastguard's role as co-ordinator and so it has a very comprehensive VHF system using many remote radio sites.

The coastguard cannot cope with every single paddler, sailor, windsurfer, power-boat user, sea angler and yachtsman who telephones them or calls them on the radio to say that they are going out for the day. However, they would like to hear from those people who operate as groups, or who are undertaking a trip, or who may be going into remote or dangerous places. Statistically, canoeists cause few problems on the sea.

If you contact the coastguard to let them know your plans, you must also have someone ashore to raise the alarm to the coastguard if a problem is suspected with your safety. The coastguard DOES NOT follow up your safe arrival! They do however log the information they receive and from this the coastguard can make a quick and effective response if needed. The person ashore should have all the details of your party and intentions, and should be the one responsible for raising the alarm if he or she becomes concerned for your party's safety. The position of responsibility that this person takes on is huge, and should not be undertaken lightly.

Some people never inform the coastguard, but if you do report in to them prior to a trip, give them the information listed opposite. It is also important to inform them of your safe return. The coastguards are friendly people who can give you information such as the latest weather forecasts, hazards in the area, tidal information, local conditions and advice. Although full time coastguards usually have maritime backgrounds, they are not all canoeists so do not expect them to understand completely the full potential of well-equipped and prepared canoes as sea-going craft. If they ask pertinent questions it is usually to your advantage – they are showing interest and concern. Both sides need to inform and educate each other. Coastguards are keen for people to get to know them. They have produced a sea canoeing safety leaflet and are also keen for canoeists to join their CG 66 Small Craft Registration Scheme previously aimed at yachtsmen, but which can be adapted for canoeists. Why not organize a visit to one of their rescue centres, listed in the telephone book.

The information that the coastguard should have:

- Number in group and where they are from.

- Canoe types and colours.

- The group's intentions with estimated times of departure (ETD) and arrival (ETA). Give emergency routes or alternatives. Will there be rescue practice or not? This is useful to know so if a member of the public reports in that canoeists have capsized, then the coastguard can refer to their log and take appropriate action. This is the same for any night-time paddling.

- What equipment is being carried? Radio, distress flares – if so, what kind, distress beacon, buoyancy aids. Is protective clothing being worn such as wetsuits or drysuits? What is the level of experience in the group? Are food and drink being carried? Do they have navigation equipment such as a compass, charts or maps? Are they equipped with any other emergency equipment? and so on.

- Is there a vehicle being used or left anywhere? Include the registration number.

Inland waterways
Rivers

As the sea can only be found surrounding our coastline, not everyone will find it easy to get to and so rivers may be more accessible. You can select a grade of difficulty of river to suit your needs. There are grades for the adrenaline junkies who want fast, exciting, turbulent rapids, with big drops to shoot, or for the more sedate and less energetic there are still, quietly moving, more peaceful rivers that conjure up images of relaxing and taking time to enjoy the scenery and wildlife. From a river you can see close at hand the actions of erosion carving channels in the earth's surface. The river passes through various transitions from its birth in the mountains from small, narrow streams which feed into progressively bigger torrents, cascading drops and waterfalls which move obstructions in its way. Turbulent youth gives way to maturity where it gets wider and deeper before flowing more sedately into the valleys and meandering at a much slower pace, depositing silt and gravel to form banks and shallows in the alluvial plains. Finally the ultimate of maturity is for the river to meet salt water in an estuary as it finds its final destination, the sea.

River access

The difficulty comes when the owner of the river may not be the owner of both the river banks. Sometimes rivers are county boundaries and different people own their respective halves of the river and bank. Sometimes fishing rights have been sold to yet another person, and still further, the control of a river may be in the hands of a Water Authority. Some rivers and their surrounding woodland may also be designated Sites of Special Scientific Interest, or be managed as National Nature Reserves which also have regulations on access. Some sections of river have navigation rights, but no access rights, so you see that the issue of access on and around inland waterways is not simple and should not be taken for granted. Please ask first by contacting the local Access Officer.

National Rivers Authority (N.R.A.)

This is an independent body set up under the Water Act of 1989 operating under regional units and is the major environmental protection agency, responsible for safeguarding and improving the natural water in England and Wales. The N.R.A. has a wide range of responsibilities for the control of the water environment including monitoring and improving the quality of water, improving and maintaining fisheries, controlling pollution, improving flood defences and warnings, conservation in water related habitats, promotion of water based recreation and promotion of navigation in some locations.

To achieve success in all these areas the N.R.A. works with industry, commerce, farmers and the general public to promote environmental awareness and to enforce the appropriate environmental standards.

River catchment and coastal areas are increasingly used for a multitude of activities. Many of these differing interests interact and inevitably some conflicts arise. The N.R.A. seeks to reconcile these conflicts and to maintain a balance between the competing requirements of all the users.

Lakes

Again depending on where you live, lakes and reservoirs may feature as part of your landscape. An attraction for lakes is that there is really only the weather to worry about and although this can be nasty and exposed, a little like the sea, at least there is a shoreline all the way round (as long as you are not somewhere like the Great Lakes in Canada, where the shore is beyond the horizon!). Most of the lakes in the UK are comparatively narrow even if they are long. One of my early experiences in the outdoors was paddling out to an island in a lake on a still, calm night with a good moon and patchy mist hovering above the water. One of the people with us was playing his flute and the sound was incredibly magical and seemed to be flowing everywhere at the same time. We could have been anywhere that night, sleeping under the stars.

The access for lakes is similar to rivers, although they seem to present less of a problem with objections from fishermen. Some lakes may have a preferred launching site if recreational boating is permitted. Reservoirs too are in a similar category to lakes, however, some encourage recreational activity with strict regulations but do not always accommodate or make provision for canoeists. Signs are usually posted at pertinent places by the water's edge or in parking places.

Canals

These may be accessible to people who cannot get to other bodies of water. The inland waterway system in England and Wales is fairly extensive. There may be the occasional sofa or car to bump into, but canals are usually more sheltered places as far as the weather is concerned, though they do carry other water-borne forms of transport such as canal barges and power-boats. Pollution is potentially a problem although many canals are being cleaned up by various groups of people.

British Waterways

British Waterways is the navigational authority for over 3,200 km (2,000 miles) of canals and river navigations in England, Scotland and Wales. About 600km (380 miles) are developed and maintained as commercial waterways for freight-carrying vessels, another 1,900km (1,200 miles) worth are the cruising waterways for boats and fishing and so on and the remaining 800km (500 miles) are maintained with due regard to safety, public health and the preservation of amenities. Of the remaining distance, two-thirds is navigable or has been restored over the past 20 years.

In order to use these waterways, a licence is required from British Waterways. The waterways are navigable by means of locks and weirs and the payment of the licence fee helps contribute towards the cost of running and maintaining them. Licences for British Waterways and a few other waterways are free to BCU members, but can be obtained from the various waterways authorities for non-members.

Canoeists' code of conduct

This code of conduct is designed to promote good relations between water users and to maintain access, so please abide by it.

Code of Conduct

- Ask and obtain permission before you use restricted areas.
- Thank people afterwards!
- Park in sensible places, even if it means paying for a car park. Do not block narrow areas and keep off grass verges.
- Be discreet when getting changed – for other people's sake.
- Pick up litter, close gates, stay on paths, do not damage crops or land.
- Obey National Trust regulations, local bye-laws and regulations for camping and caravanning.
- Keep away from banks from which people are fishing.
- Please keep the peace.

Central Council for Physical Recreation (CCPR) canoeing code

This is a canoeing code more explicitly aimed at the canoeist than other water users:

CCPR Canoeing Code

- Keep clear of fishermen in all respects: their lines, the banks they are on and the fishing pools; do not cause a disturbance; comply with their signals if they wish you to wait and so on.
- As far as other vessels are concerned, canoeists should give way to larger and less manoeuvrable craft. Canoes can move easily into shallower water. Rowing craft may also have difficulty in spotting canoeists, so keep well clear.

4

Safety

So long as our evolutionary development requires us to breathe air in order to survive, then there will always be inherent risks with any water based activity, such as canoeing.

Life is full of risks and so is canoeing. That is what makes canoeing exciting and challenging. Some of the risks are obvious, like canoeing over waterfalls, or capsizing and swimming down a nasty rapid. Others are less obvious but potentially as serious, such as going out alone, not wearing enough warm clothing, changes in the weather, cold and hungry paddlers with no warm drink or food available, not checking your equipment, being put under pressure by friends to do something you are not comfortable with and so on.

Safety is about minimizing risks. It is not about making lists of 'dos and don'ts'. Being safe is being aware of the dangers and taking the necessary precautions to guard against them before they happen. People who are trained and well prepared can have fun and excitement in challenging situations where an untrained or inexperienced person could drown.

To reduce unnecessary risks you need to be able to recognize their potential for developing and learn the skills you will need to perform in the event of adverse circumstances. If you analyse incidents that have occurred in the past (and will no doubt occur in the future) you will find that few mistakes on their own are life-threatening, but several mistakes made together can leave things open to the possibility of a serious problem.

In life we all take risks and we all make mistakes, but we need to be able to recognize when they are mounting up and leading to the potential for disaster. If you anticipate what could possibly go wrong and are prepared for it, then if ever such a situation should occur, you will be better able to deal with it effectively. You cannot always be prepared for everything, but you can do your best.

As mentioned earlier in this book, the best way to learn to canoe is with other people who are suitably experienced. Getting out on the water safely in the right place, at the right time, with the right people and the right equipment, without overestimating your ability may sound unexciting, but you will live to repeat it. Between 1989 and 1992, on what is considered to be very 'easy' water, the canoe fatalities which occurred seem to show a correlation between inexperience and not wearing personal buoyancy.

There are lots of questions that you should ask yourself (and answer honestly) before taking to the water. Even if you are on a beginner's canoe course, by asking these questions you can see how other people prepare for canoeing activities and so begin to educate yourself. Education is an important part of paddling.

Ask yourself:

- Can you swim?
- Do you have the right personal equipment?
- Have you got the necessary skill level for what you are doing?
- What experience do you have? Is it relevant?
- Do you know what hazards are involved in what you are doing?
- Are you prepared for (and do you have) equipment for an emergency?
- Is what you are doing your idea or someone else's?
- Is your canoe safe enough for what you intend to do?
- Does anyone else know what you are doing or where you are going?

Fear of capsize

It is natural to be afraid of capsizing and being stuck in your kayak. A good way to come to terms with this fear is to play lots of games in, and on top of, swamped boats and so on. Practising capsizing will help you to come to terms with fears and anxieties, can also be fun and will help you gain confidence and increase your ability as you come to know what to expect. Being relaxed with your canoe is important. Take your canoe for a swim and see how it responds.

Looking after your equipment

Taking care of your equipment is an important aspect of safety. If you look after your equipment it will serve you well when you most need it.

Remember, one mistake on its own is not normally fatal. Recognize the potential for mistakes to build up – not looking after equipment is one.

Examples of not looking after equipment include:

• Using your buoyancy aid for anything other than it was intended, such as sitting on it, or using it as protective padding for your canoe. All this does is put wear and tear on your most vital piece of equipment and it may seriously damage it. I used my buoyancy aid once to protect the hull of my loaded sea kayak on a trailer when transporting it up from the beach on a really bumpy track. One of the narrow strips of flotation broke in half, no doubt reducing its effectiveness.

• Sitting on your canoe while it is on the shore can damage the seams and hull, because body weight compresses the boat when it is on the ground. When the canoe is on the water, the water provides support for it in all the right places. You may not notice the damage, especially if it is made of fibreglass but even polyethylene boats can be severely gouged or dented if treated in this way.

• Sea water and grit or dirt of any form needs to be rinsed off everything. Sea water is a good corrosive and grit and dirt get into and jam movable fittings.

Do not compromise yourself and others by poorly looked after equipment and think 'It will be all right, just this once'. You may find that your equipment is not as effective as it ought to be just when you most need it to be.

Safety equipment that you should carry

Good practice is to carry enough equipment to use or improvize with in the event of an emergency. This may depend on what you are going to do, where you are going, how long you will be out and the time of year.

You should include such things as: extra food (chocolate), a means of making a hot drink (flask or stove, with fuel, water, matches and flavouring ingedients), high insulation spare clothing, a means of making an emergency shelter (bivvy bag or exposure bag), a first aid kit, a small repair kit (knife, string, sylglass (see page 49) duct tape, nuts and bolts for foot rests), a means of towing a canoe (towline and clip for attaching to canoe) and whistles. Each person in the party should also ensure that they have adequate personal clothing, including waterproof and wind-proof layers for themselves.

Waterproof containers

Keeping everything dry is a big challenge. There are two basic kinds of waterproof containers: rigid or semi-rigid containers that have waterproof lids and waterproof bags.

Rigid or semi-rigid containers

These come in a variety of shapes and sizes and they are useful for carrying such things as cameras, repair kits, first aid kits, and anything else that is fragile, has sharp edges that need protecting, or you do not want to be squashed. These containers are durable but bulky.

Waterproof bags

These are better for maximizing space as they can be squeezed into small places. Several small ones are better than large ones, and better for obtaining a more even weight distribution.

Smaller, rigid containers with screw-on lids

This is about the size of a rucksack

'Soft', small waterproof bags

A large, rigid container

Twist this section

To seal up plastic bags, roll the top from one side to the other, squeezing ALL the air out as you go

Fold the top part down and seal with elastic

4.1 Waterproof containers come in various sizes and types with different methods of closure on top. Any container is suitable for an open canoes, but only the smaller ones are suitable for kayaks.

Rip-proof nylon bags which, when lined with a well-sealed polythene bag, are effective, cheap substitutes for the more expensive, but durable heavy-duty waterproof bags.

Whatever the container however, experience has taught me never to rely on them being 100 per cent waterproof. I always use a good quality, heavy gauge plastic bag as a liner, even inside the more expensive bags, with strong elastic (called shock-cord) or car inner-tube for sealing up their tops.

What equipment to pack where?

Knowing what equipment you have put where, and in what container, is important especially with safety equipment, so that you can find what you want when you want it. A combination of containers is therefore useful.

The equipment should be packed so that the heavier items are as close to the centre of the canoe as possible. This makes turning and manoeuvring easier. There should never be anything loose in the boat. Everything should be tied in or firmly secured, and nothing should be in the way of the area in which you sit or kneel.

Remember that, despite the canoe being much slower to respond with all the extra equipment, the bags add to the internal buoyancy because they are airtight and will keep water out should you capsize.

Repairing canoes

The kind of repair kit that you need will depend on your canoe and what material it is made of. Looking after your equipment is the best prevention that you can do. However, there always comes a time when you will need to fix something.

Temporary repairs

Temporary repairs to canoes still on the water, with holes or cracks in them, can be done best by using plumber's tape or 'Sylglass', available from hardware stores.

It comes in large rolls, with or without a foil backing and is about 5cm (2in) wide. Although it is messy to handle and not very aesthetic it makes a good, short-term repair. The great advantage with Sylglass is that it will stick to anything, wet or dry. A small hole can be filled and covered with the tape inside and out and a larger hole can be covered with a piece of more rigid plastic, from containers such as catering size squash bottles, then sealed with the tape on both sides.

Handling Sylglass (plumber's tape)

The best way of handling sylglass is to prepare pre-cut strips of about 15cm (6in) in length and lay them between two pieces of plastic bag, which are then trimmed all the way round to within about 2cm (1in) of the tape. Roll these strips up and they are then ready for use. Peel off one side of the plastic, put the tape onto the canoe where you need it, and press the tape down firmly through the other piece of plastic, which is then removed when you have finished. This way you stand less chance of getting your hands messy. You could also carry polythene gloves.

Duct tape

Duct tape (or carpet tape) is also a universal tape used, in the short-term, for repairing anything that is dry: canoes, paddles, tents and other equipment that has holes, tears or breaks. Similarly it has proved very versatile for people who need patching up for scrapes, blisters, slings and so on, and is therefore a must for all repair kits. Duct tape is available from hardware stores in various sized rolls.

Permanent repairs
Fibreglass

For more permanent repairs a fibreglass canoe is easily patched with resin-soaked pieces of chopped strand mat, but this does require a dry, warm environment. The area around the patch will first need roughing up with a grinder or equivalent, to allow the patch to stick properly. Make sure you wear a mask, goggles and ear protection.

Polyethylene

Repairing polyethylene canoes can be more difficult. Linear polyethylene can be heat welded, but some canoes are made of cross-linked plastic which is harder to damage and harder to repair. A number of manufacturers and retailers offer a repair service.

ABS (Acrylonitrile-butadiene-styrene)

ABS canoes are incredibly robust and are also difficult to repair. Among other uses, the very slippery, hard-wearing outer plastic covering is also used for protecting the layers underneath from ultraviolet damage (a good reason for not dragging your canoe over abrasive surfaces). If this outer layer of plastic is damaged (that is only the colour disappears) then it can be covered with fibreglass and polyester resin. Kevlar and polyester resin are also good for making a 'bang plate' on the keel-line at the bow, both above and below the waterline, for preventing surface damage in this vulnerable area.

You need to find out what materials your canoe is made of and which types of resins and catalyst hardeners they are compatible with. If they are not compatible then the resin and catalyst may well eat up or dissolve materials, such as the foam in the walls of your canoe. ABS is a styrene-based plastic so polyester resin is all right. Royalex repairs can be made with epoxy resin repair kits that include 'putty' for outside scratches.

The manufacturers are the best people to ask for advice. I have seen a few deep gouges in the hulls of these canoes, but I have not as yet seen one of them holed, even after seeing the results of an open canoe that was constantly used as a 'wrap boat' to pin against obstructions for practising white water rescues.

Aluminium

Open canoes made of aluminium usually dent if they hit something hard. This can be straightened out best by being knocked back into place. Just beware of the limitations that an alloy has in terms of metal fatigue, if the same place is damaged repeatedly. Pop riveting or welding may be other alternatives for repairing worse damage.

The advice for long-term repair is to look after your boats and prevent unnecessary damage, as much as possible, and then they will probably out-last you or your use for them.

5

First aid

It is impossible to cover all aspects of emergency first aid in this book. Some basic principles of what to do in an emergency will be covered in this chapter in the hope that you will take the responsibility yourself to extend your knowledge and training in this vital area.

There is no substitute for training and attending wilderness related first aid or life-saving courses. I recommend for further reading the *Outward Bound First Aid Handbook*.

Being away from immediate medical services is an integral part of outdoor activities such as canoeing, and the ability to deal with an accident under such circumstances is paramount. The more training and practice you do, the more familiar you become with what to do in an emergency, such as capsizing and rescues.

There are few aspects of first aid that are unique to canoeing. Wherever you are the same skills and treatment are required of most medical conditions, regardless of the activity. Practice and training can help you cope with the emotional stress in dealing with the injuries, as well as providing the confidence necessary to respond effectively in emergency situations.

Establishing priorities

Your first priority is NOT first aid! Before charging off to deal with a situation, you need to make sure that neither you nor anyone else will become another casualty.

Once you have established that the situation is safe for all concerned, then you can make an assessment of the injury. The way you organize your response to an incident is vital to make sure you get all the right information to assess the casualty's condition.

Your first priorities in any rescue situation, in this order, are to:

- Protect yourself.
- Protect the rest of the party.
- Protect the patient.

Organizing your response

This is a useful sequence to help you organize yourself in collecting information, identifying problems and making a plan to deal with each one. It is also the same order in which medical records and information are noted and passed on.

1) **Subjective information** or the 'story' obtained from the casualty or others. What happened? 'I fell three feet and landed here, on my knee.' What do they complain of and tell you about their symptoms? 'It hurts here when I try to move it and I can't put my weight on it.' Other important medical information to obtain is known factors such as allergies, diabetes and medication being taken, and things like the weather or cold water which may disguise the symptoms or make them worse.

2) **Objective information** or what you find in your examination – tenderness, swelling, bruising and so on. Make sure you see and feel everything to be sure nothing is missed. What are their vital signs? Their pulse rate, breathing rate, level of consciousness (use the AVPU scale: A = Awake, V = responding to someone's Voice, P = only responding to Pain and U = Unresponsive). What is their skin like? Its colour (pink, pale), temperature (warm, cool) and moisture (dry, sweaty). Also write down the time at which all of these are taken.

3) Your **Assessment** and anticipated problems should be based on the findings mentioned above and a decision made as to their severity relative to each other. Anticipated problems are what the injury could lead to over time. For example a person who has been unconscious but is now conscious and awake (on the AVPU scale) is still at risk and will need careful monitoring for at least the next

24 hours, in case signs and symptoms of a head injury develop.

4) Your **Plan** or what you are going to do to help treat each problem and your plan for getting the casualty to medical help.

If you take the first letter from each stage above they spell SOAP and a written up 'SOAP' example is as follows:

S – Subjective information: A 14-year-old boy slipped and caught his ankle between some rocks. He complains of pain in his right ankle and tingling in his toes. He has no complaints of pain anywhere else.

O – Objective: An awake (AVPU scale) and orientated boy is suffering from discomfort. The right ankle is swollen and tender to the touch. He refuses to move his ankle of his own accord. His toes are warm and pink and can be wiggled, although pain is felt at his ankle. He can feel the touch of a twig on the end of each toe and he has no other apparent injuries.

A – Assessment: Fracture of the right ankle.

P – Plan: Splint ankle. Monitor tingling, colour and feeling of toes, and transport to hospital.

The notes present a clear picture of the situation, who the casualty is, what happened and what is going to be done.

Expired air resuscitation
Artificial respiration
In any canoeing accident the most serious, life-threatening incident that you are likely to come across is drowning or suffocation. Artificial respiration is the treatment for people who have stopped breathing. It can usually be done immediately and in just about any position or location. The critical thing is that it is done without delay, as soon as the casualty's face is above the water. Early artificial respiration will prevent a casualty who has stopped breathing, which is easy to treat, from deteriorating into a worse condition where his or her heart stops beating, which is not so easy to treat. Artificial respiration is a proven successful life-saving procedure and will keep someone alive if it is done quickly. Breathing stops before the heart stops.

Near drowning

Drowning usually refers to death due to failure of the ability to breathe, because water gets in the way of the vital gas exchanges that occur in the lungs. The term 'near drowning' indicates survival, at least for the time being. However, lungs contaminated with water need not always be fatal, but survival will depend on the amount of water they have in them. The most common form of drowning is the loss of muscular co-ordination due to cold water which quickly suppresses the person's ability to swim so the casualty sinks and inhales water.

Drowning can also happen almost instantly with the gasp of surprise on entering cold water causing the casualty to suck water into the airway and, the brain being deprived of oxygen, will quickly cause the casualty to lose consciousness. In medical facilities with advanced life-support equipment rare cases (particularly children) have been resuscitated after submersion in cold water for up to one hour with little or no long-term brain damage. After an hour, however, with no more oxygen left to maintain the reflex which stops water entering the lungs, the reflex relaxes and lets water in. This reflex also seems to disappear as we get older.

The treatment for someone who has been recovered from the water and is not breathing, is artificial respiration. There is no need to attempt to drain the lungs, because the water that enters them is absorbed a bit like sponges, and so will not readily drain out. The water that you see coming out of the mouth is not from the lungs but from the stomach.

Also take into account the fact that the casualty may be suffering from hypothermia and be certain that there is no pulse before initiating heart compressions. Most people who survive drowning have a beating heart and respond to artificial respiration within the first couple of minutes, while a pulse is still being searched for. Those who do not have a pulse on recovery from the water have a lower chance of survival.

Anyone who has been 'recovered' from a near drowning MUST

go to hospital as soon as possible. Water is an irritant to the tissues in the lung and can cause the onset of further complications within the respiratory system, which may be delayed for 24 to 72 hours.

Cardio-pulmonary resuscitation (CPR)

Cardio-pulmonary resuscitation (CPR) is a combination of chest compressions and artificial respiration, the outlines of which can be found in the British Red Cross, St John Ambulance or St Andrew's Ambulance Association courses.

In the wild, away from immediate medical help, CPR has a limited value. The casualty's own natural heartbeat must be regained within a short period of time if the casualty is to survive. This usually requires advanced medical aid which uses drugs and electrical defibrillation.

Breathing for someone can be of use for hours or days but chest compressions cannot support circulation of the blood for a prolonged period of time. Most medical authorities agree that the chances of a casualty's survival are minimal if spontaneous heart activity is not restored within 30 minutes. The EXCEPTIONS to this are in cases of severe hypothermia (see page 64) and cold water drowning (see page 55).

The purpose of CPR

The purpose of CPR is to maintain life by slowing down the dying process of the brain. This will hopefully buy enough time to get the casualty to advanced medical aid, so that life-support treatment can be administered.

A person who is not breathing, may still have a heartbeat. If the 'not breathing' is not treated immediately, the heart will quickly stop. If the heart stops then immediate CPR needs to be performed. Breathing for the casualty can be done in any position, but heart compressions must have a firm horizontal surface first. Early attempts at starting full CPR without a firm surface are a waste of time.

A = Airway   B = Breathing   C = Circulation – pulse
                                                         – bleeding

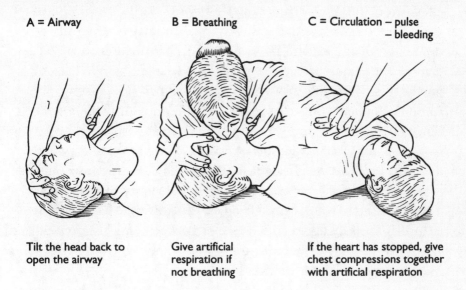

Tilt the head back to   Give artificial   If the heart has stopped, give
open the airway   respiration if   chest compressions together
                           not breathing   with artificial respiration

5.1 The ABC of resuscitation.

Performing artificial respiration and CPR

In your examination of the casualty check for the three important
things first: A = AIRWAY, B = BREATHING and C = CIRCULA-
TION. Without immediate attention to these the casualty will not
survive. The priority in which you assess these is A B C, the
Airway first, then breathing and then circulation which has two
aspects; pulse and blood loss.

A – AIRWAY Check for breathing. Place your head near the
casualty's mouth and nose. Listen and feel for air movement on
your face, cheeks or lips while you look for any movement of the
chest or water vapour condensing around the mouth.

If there is no breathing, there may be a problem with the airway, or a problem with the ability to breathe so open the airway.
To do this, lift the chin, which tilts the head backwards and lifts
the tongue away from the back of the casualty's throat. If they
still do not breathe, then breathe for them. Any obstruction
which blocks air going in will prevent resuscitation. Remove

helmet chin-straps, loosen clothing and reposition the airway. If air goes in, the problem is not the airway, but is B – BREATH-ING. If repositioning of the airway and the first few breaths do not allow air in, assume the cause of the obstruction to be foreign material and clear the airway. This is done by hand, using gravity first. Roll the casualty onto his or her side keeping the spine in line and 'finger sweep' round the mouth. If there is no potential for spinal injury then roll the casualty onto his or her front and put your hands underneath his or her middle (waist) and pull up. This is effective in clearing any vomit. However if you suspect there is a potential for spinal injury and a 'finger sweep' of the mouth is not effective then the safest compromise is to roll the casualty onto his or her back keeping the spine in line. Place the heel of your hand just below the chest and perform a sharp thrust towards the chest.

This is the Heimlich manoeuvre and uses air still in the lungs to force any obstruction out of the airway. It may need repeating, and do not forget to check the airway and remove any obstruction subsequently released.

B – BREATHING Even if the airway is open the casualty may not be able to breathe adequately. Inadequate breathing means that there is not enough air moving in and out to support life, which means that breathing is absent, very slow, or very irregular. If you have any doubt, breathe for them. If they are conscious, speak to them, as a person who can speak, generally has adequate breathing.

To perform artificial respiration, pinch the casualty's nostrils and seal your lips on the casualty's mouth. Give two quick inflations. Then inflate at a rate of about 12–16 breaths per minute, one every 5 seconds or so. The amount is adequate when you see the chest rising slightly. Take about 1–1½ seconds per breath. Breathing faster than this generally blows air into the stomach and leads to vomiting. Watch the chest rise and then deflate for each inhalation. When the casualty is breathing normally, put him or her into the recovery position.

C – CIRCULATION has two aspects 1) pulse, 2) bleeding. PULSE A stopped heart immediately leads to a loss of consciousness and no breathing. A person who is awake, or responds to sound or pain, or is breathing or moving spontaneously has a heart that is beating. Pulses can be very difficult to find due to cold hands or fear, as well as the pulse being very weak or slow. The artery in the neck, the carotid has the easiest pulse to get to and the strongest pulse to feel. If this pulse is absent the heart is not beating.

If there is no pulse start CPR. Make sure the airway is open and check there is no spontaneous breathing. Give two quick inflations. Check that there is no carotid pulse. A single sharp blow to the centre of the sternum may restart the heart. Check again for a restored pulse. Place the casualty horizontally, or slightly head-down, on a firm surface, remove their buoyancy aid and necessary clothing to feel the bottom of their breast-bone. Find the bottom of the breast-bone between the ribs, and measure two fingers' width up from the bottom of it by placing two fingers on the breast bone. Put the heel of one hand on the breast-bone right next to the fingers and put your other hand on top of the first. Interlock your fingers and pull them up and away from the chest.

Keeping your arms straight, lean your body weight right over the chest to press down vertically on the breast-bone to move it 4–5cm (1½–2in), compressing slightly faster than one per second ('one and two and three...') and releasing pressure without removing your hands. Repeat the compressions aiming for about 80 a minute.

To combine chest compressions with artificial respiration, give two breaths, then 15 compressions, return to two breaths and repeat with a ratio of 15 to 2 until help arrives. (With children increase the rates of compression and inflation and apply less pressure.) If there are two people available, one should start CPR while the other goes for help, then work on CPR together at a rate of five compressions to one breath. If the pulse recovers before breathing, continue artificial respiration. If both pulse and breathing are restarted, but the casualty remains unconscious, place the casualty in the recovery position and monitor his or her breathing.

Dealing with an unconscious, breathing casualty

Whatever caused the loss of consciousness, treating this condition is always a priority. A common cause of death in unconscious people is the inhalation of such things as water, food, blood or the tongue into the back of the throat, where it will prevent air getting into the lungs and cause suffocation. The most important thing you can probably do as a first aider is to monitor the airway and keep it open from the moment that you start treating the casualty and throughout the whole recovery – one person should do nothing else but keep the airway open.

Rest while partner performs artificial respiration

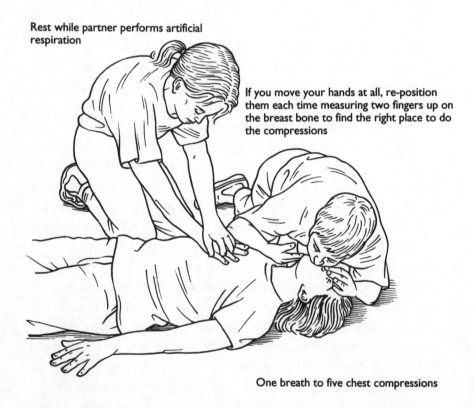

If you move your hands at all, re-position them each time measuring two fingers up on the breast bone to find the right place to do the compressions

One breath to five chest compressions

5.2 Resuscitation for two people.

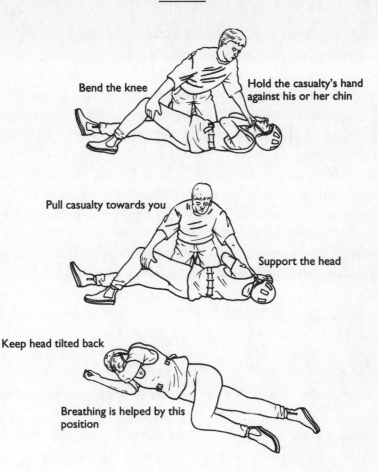

Bend the knee

Hold the casualty's hand against his or her chin

Pull casualty towards you

Support the head

Keep head tilted back

Breathing is helped by this position

5.3 Putting a breathing and unconscious casualty into the recovery position.

The recovery position

The recovery position prevents the tongue from falling back into the throat blocking the airway and also allows drainage of any other substances away from it. You must still monitor the airway. An unconscious patient should never be left alone on their back.

BLEEDING The loss of blood if not stopped and treated leads to shock and possibly death. Bleeding can be external and obvious or internal and more difficult to find. External bleeding may be missed if a full examination is not done, as bulky clothing or lots of clothing may conceal and absorb the blood. If the casualty is in the water for any amount of time, the water will just wash the blood away. There is no easy measure for deciding when bleeding is severe. A general rule is that if it looks like there is a lot of blood loss, then it probably is.

All bleeding will stop in time, either because the casualty has no more blood left or because it has been controlled. External bleeding is controlled with well-aimed, direct pressure. If the bleeding continues despite the direct pressure, remove the dressing and locate the EXACT source of the bleeding and re-aim your pressure. The clotting process takes ten minutes or more to occur, so continue to apply pressure until the bleeding is controlled.

Internal bleeding will not often be detected in the initial examination and unless you take the casualty's vital signs and know what to look for in the vital sign trends you may not detect internal bleeding at all.

Severe internal bleeding can usually be associated with an accident which has potential for causing injury to the chest, abdomen, femur (thigh bone) and pelvis (hip). Internal bleeding requires surgery and urgent transport to a medical facility.

The body's response to the cold and hypothermia

The body has natural functions which allow it to compensate for the effect that a cold environment can have on it. The body has the ability to retain what heat it has and reduce heat that it is losing to the environment. When these functions are working, the body's temperature is normal at 37°C (98.6°F). The body's natural functions: reduce the amount of blood flowing to the skin and extremities (the limbs); cause the body to shiver, which may or may not be present; and increase the urine output as it is harder for the body to heat up any excess liquid so you need to urinate more frequently. The person who is cold and NOT yet hypothermic is awake and alert, his levels of consciousness are normal, he has a pale, cool skin, feels uncomfortably cold and is shivering either slightly or very obviously.

No specific treatment is required at this stage, as the body is compensating for the cold. However, a balance must be maintained between reducing the cold environment and increasing the body's heat production as further changes in the environment, or limited food and fluid may overpower the body's ability to compensate, resulting in hypothermia. The body needs food and fluid before being able to increase its own heat production.

Mild hypothermia

This occurs when there is an imbalance between the body's own heat production and the cold environment. The body's ability to compensate has been over-powered and its temperature has fallen to between 35°C–32°C (95°F–90°F). This can occur quickly if immersed in cold water, or slowly over hours or days. Most drownings occur because the body's extremities lose their ability to co-ordinate as the body takes blood from them to keep other more vital organs warm. Someone who has been partly or completely submerged in cold water for a period of time may quickly reach the stage where they are totally unresponsive, having shown no earlier signs or symptoms of hypothermia at all.

Recognizing the early signs is imperative. Treat the early signs by reducing the cold. Get out of the wind and water. Put on plenty of dry clothing. Warm the environment and retain what heat the body already has. Give warm liquids and fast acting calories from simple sugars such as chocolate and sweets. Induce exercise as long as there is enough food and liquid in the body and the exercise does not further increase the risk of exposure to the cold environment.

Mild hypothermia needs urgent recognition and treatment. As the body's temperature drops, complex processes take place in the body which, unless stopped and reversed, will lead the casualty into severe hypothermia with decreased levels of consciousness, then unconsciousness and ultimately, death.

Severe hypothermia

Severe lowering of the body temperature is a form of hibernation. The body's ability to 'hibernate' like this can protect and preserve itself for a significant but limited amount of time after which these 'hibernating' systems will cease to function.

As the body temperature drops below 32°C (90°F) the casualty will probably display, for them, unusual behaviour or personality traits. Shivering will also stop, speech will become almost impossible, as will trying to stand up. These symptoms will combine with, and be followed by, a decrease in the casualty's state of consciousness on the AVPU scale from Awake and confused, to responding to Voice, responding to Pain, through to Unresponsive. This change is very different from the lethargic, but responsive person in the early stages of mild hypothermia.

Distinguishing between mild and severe hypothermia is important for treatment away from medical facilities. Re-warming a severely hypothermic casualty in the field can be dangerous as there is great potential for several serious repercussions. The casualty should NOT be exercised. He or she should be transported to a medical facility quickly and VERY GENTLY as sudden movements can irritate the now cold and sensitive heart and cause it to stop. When monitoring a pulse in severe hypothermia, it may be weak and as slow as one beat per minute making it difficult to feel. So take the pulse for at least a minute. If you initiate CPR on a cold but beating heart you could cause it to stop. However, breathe for them if their breathing is inadequate. When you transport them ensure that they are flat and wrapped up well to prevent further heat loss. Severe hypothermia is a serious condition which is best prevented by early recognition and treatment.

6

Going afloat

Transporting canoes

A lot of damage can occur to canoes that are badly transported on roof-racks and trailers.

If they are not tied down properly they not only damage themselves when jettisoned, but potentially could damage everything else in their flightpath too, such as people and property. They can also be damaged by being tied down too tightly, as fibreglass seams can split and polyethylene canoes can develop depressions. The balance to aim for is somewhere between security and being over cautious.

Kayaks generally travel well in any position but some are better transported hull down. However this is specific to more specialized kayaks. For example I would not like to put my sea kayak (an Anus Acuta) upside down on a roof-rack because the seams could be damaged as the front deck is quite rounded. It travels better on its hull or its side.

You can buy bolt-on J- bars or V-bars which attach to standard roof-racks to take the kayaks and prevent any sideways movement of the kayak. These bar attachments are also kinder to the boats, offering protection from damage.

Open canoes travel best upside down on their gunwales, but check their ground clearance on a trailer before you drive off. Make sure also, that if you put them on your roof-rack upside down, you can see out of the windscreen.

If you are at all superstitious and would like every ounce of good luck in your favour then ensure your canoe travels bow first facing forwards. It is reputed to be a bad omen for a canoe to travel backwards!

Tying canoes down

Now that you have decided on your beliefs, it is time to tie the boat down.

Transporting a canoe on a roof-rack

- Check the roof-rack and that its points of attachment are in good condition. Tests prove that even in low-speed impacts badly secured roof-racks can be torn off, making a lethal projectile.

- If you are not very good at tying knots, then treat yourself to some straps that come with self-locking buckles. (See figure 6.1 on knots overleaf.)

- Make sure that you have either taken everything out of the canoe, or that whatever is inside is securely attached to it. Things such as sponges, spray-decks, vacuum flasks, throwbags and so on, all make good pickings for those lucky (or unlucky depending on the damage) recipients of wind and gravity distribution!

- If you have a long way to go and the kayak is sitting on its hull the right way up, put the spray-deck on and tie up the waist tube with elastic or rope. It will more than likely rain and a kayak with water inside it increases the weight on the roof considerably.

- Tie the ends of the canoes to the front and rear of the car too, so that if the worst should happen, you are not just relying on the roof-rack clamps to hold the canoes in place.

- If you have your canoe insured and you intend to leave it on the roof-rack unguarded for any amount of time, you might want to buy a lock for it which goes around the seat and is clamped to the inside of the car door.

Transporting a canoe on a trailer

- Attach a strong loop of chain or wire from the trailer near the tow-hitch to the vehicle to prevent run-away trailers if the vehicle and trailer should become separated for any reason.

- Leave enough of a gap between the boats and the back of the vehicle for tight corners and reversing.

- Check the balance of the trailer. Two people should easily be able to lift the tongue by the tow-hitch.

- When tying the boats down, as on the roof-rack, to stop them shooting forwards thread a rope from the trailer through the grab handles/toggles and back to the trailer. Alternatively secure each boat in this way. This is made easier for open canoes if they have their painters attached to strong places.

- The socket for the lights is usually damaged while fitting and removing. Let it be the last thing you connect to the vehicle and the first you take off!

- Check that all the lights work and they are visible.

- Make sure that the trailer has a registration plate the same as the towing vehicle.

- Carry a spare tyre.

- Remember that you are towing a trailer!

The law in the UK requires that if anything overhangs your vehicle:

- Up to 1.83m (6ft) that 'it must be clearly identified'. This can mean with a brightly coloured cloth tied to the end of it.

- Over 1.83m (6ft) that 'it must be clearly identified with warning triangles at the side and rear of the object'.

If you have not given up by now and you have finally got to your destination, here are some tips on ways to carry your canoe to the launching site.

Carrying canoes

If your canoe is heavy or it is windy and you do not want to know what it is like to be a gyroscope, then having someone to

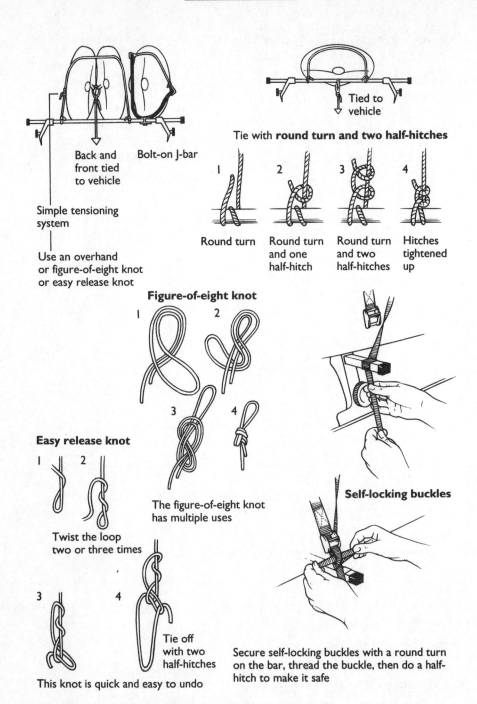

Back and front tied to vehicle

Bolt-on J-bar

Simple tensioning system

Use an overhand or figure-of-eight knot or easy release knot

Tied to vehicle

Tie with **round turn and two half-hitches**

1 — Round turn

2 — Round turn and one half-hitch

3 — Round turn and two half-hitches

4 — Hitches tightened up

Figure-of-eight knot

1   2   3   4

The figure-of-eight knot has multiple uses

Easy release knot

1   2

Twist the loop two or three times

3   4

Tie off with two half-hitches

This knot is quick and easy to undo

Self-locking buckles

Secure self-locking buckles with a round turn on the bar, thread the buckle, then do a half-hitch to make it safe

6.1 Tying canoes onto roof-racks and trailers.

Carrying a kayak like a suitcase for short distances. Suitable for light canoes

Carrying a kayak on your shoulder is better for longer distances

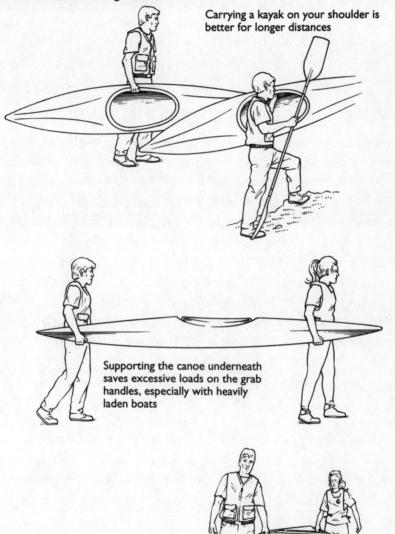

Supporting the canoe underneath saves excessive loads on the grab handles, especially with heavily laden boats

Carrying an open canoe upright. Hold onto the inside of the gunwales on opposite sides. Put your paddles in the canoe

6.2 Methods of carrying boats.

help is much more preferable. For very short distances kayaks can be carried by holding the cockpit at its balance point a bit like carrying a suitcase. For longer distances though carrying it on your shoulder is better. Beware of damaging your back when lifting heavy loads. Lift carefully by bending your knees and keeping your back straight.

Open canoe – solo lift and carry

Open canoes vary in weight depending on the size and the materials used. Some can weigh about 39kg (85lbs) for example, so be careful. When you attempt this lift have someone standing by ready to help you to both lift and lower the canoe if you need it.

Having a fitted portage yoke, which is a centre thwart shaped with a curve in the middle, is best. Then to make carrying it any distance more comfortable, pad the yoke with clothing unless you are lucky and have well developed, bulging muscles on the shoulders or your own portage pads. Portage pads are bolt-on blocks of padding mounted on a piece of wood that clamp onto the thwart and can be adjusted for your shoulder width.

Going with the laws of superstition, as explained earlier, the curve on the centre thwart faces forwards, so when the canoe is lifted onto your shoulders the curve of the centre thwart follows the natural curve of your shoulders and neck. To get ready to lift the canoe up stand at the centre of the canoe and turn it away from you onto its side so that the hull is resting against your legs. Spread your feet apart for better balance. Keeping your back straight and bending your knees, lift the canoe up so that it rests on your thighs.

With the canoe in balance like this, move your arm nearest the bow to the far side of the centre thwart, your arm nearest the stern can then hold either of two places depending on your preference: hold the near side of the centre thwart by the gunwale; or cradle the side of the canoe nearest you between your knees.

Then with a rocking motion, swing, roll and lift the canoe up and over your head so that the portage yoke ends up on your

Tip canoe onto its side

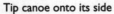

Keep your back straight and bend
your knees while supporting the
canoe on your thighs

Swing, roll and lift the canoe up
over your head

Balance the canoe. You may need
to tie something light to the inside
of the boat at one end to get the
balance right for you

6.3 Open canoe – solo lift.

shoulders, balancing it so that you can see where you are going. Carrying is made easier if the canoe is slightly heavier in the stern because you can rest your hands on the inside of the gunwales to pull it down a little. You may prefer to have a paddle or small item of kit tied to one end of the canoe for better balance. A well balanced canoe is much easier to carry.

Lowering the open canoe

Putting the canoe down can be more hazardous. You need to ensure that your head is clear of anything likely to trap it when you reverse the procedure. This may sound obvious but injuries do occur, especially if you have fitted the portage pads too close together and only left a small gap for your head. Ensure you lift the canoe well clear of your head and your ears! Lower the canoe onto your thighs and then to the ground (or get someone to help you do this).

Alternatively find a suitable place high enough on which to rest the bow, so that you can escape from underneath and then lower the canoe.

Open canoe – two person lift and carry

There are probably many different ways of doing this but the principles are the same as in the solo lift. Using two people to lift the heavier open canoes, however, is easier.

First decide who is going to carry the canoe. This person stands closer to the centre of the canoe. You both need to lift the bow up together with the stern on the ground either as in the solo lift or by facing each other, sideways on to the canoe and reaching for the gunwales with your hands. You should reach for the near gunwale with the nearest hand and the further gunwale with the other hand. Keep your feet far enough apart for good balance, then swing, roll and lift the canoe above your heads. The person who is going to carry the canoe then moves backwards into the portage position under the centre thwart and yoke. The other person takes the weight of the boat by holding the bow in the air.

Putting the canoe back down is just a reverse of this procedure. Place the stern on the ground and the person helping bears the weight in the bow as described above, so the person who carried the canoe can escape from underneath and then help lower the canoe to the ground.

Basic canoeing techniques
Holding the paddles
Your hands should grip the paddle a little wider than shoulder width apart. The grip is naturally quite wide and you will undoubtedly modify this slightly as time progresses.

Kayak
Hold the paddles a bit wider than shoulder width apart and equal distance from each end of the blade. Your 'fixed' hand or 'control' hand will always grip the paddle, while the other hand will allow the shaft to rotate in it (like revving the throttle on a motor bike), so decide which hand is going to be your control hand. This side will put the blade in the water first. To avoid confusion this description is for a right-handed control hand.

The knuckles of your control hand (right) should line up with the vertical blade on the right. If the shaft is oval you will be able to feel this position easily. This ensures that the blade on your control side (right) is always at the same angle when you put it in the water. Doing a practice drill will help you get the feel of the movement. Stand in the water up to about knee depth, or have a good imagination and do it on dry land. Put your control hand (right) blade into the water and pull it back to your hip, as if it was your hand in the water and you were swimming, doing front crawl.

Lift the blade out of the water when it reaches your hips. When the blade comes out, your control hand (right) opens the throttle, your wrist drops and pushes forward rotating your knuckles backwards. The left hand relaxes and allows the shaft to swivel to the correct position before gripping, with the knuckles

Lift the blade out of the water

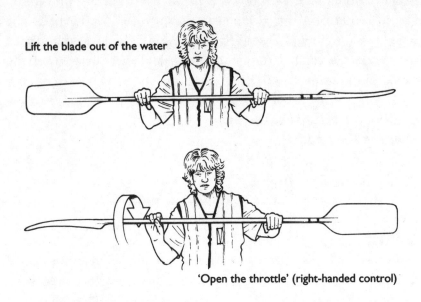

'Open the throttle' (right-handed control)

6.4 Feathering the paddle.

in line with the blade, ready to repeat on the other side. This action of turning the blades is called 'feathering'. Once you have feathered the blades, put the left blade in the water and pull back to the hip. Lift the left blade out of the water.

Swivel the shaft again so that the right blade is ready to enter the water again. Your control hand (right) should not have moved its position on the shaft at all. The left hand holds the shaft loosely letting it swivel, until the blade is in the correct position, with the knuckles in line with the edge of the vertical blade again.

Those who prefer their left hand as the control hand, grip with their left hand and allow the shaft to swivel loosely in their right. To describe this action is more complicated than it is to actually do it.

Take note that most of the stroke's power comes from just the first few inches of the stroke when the paddle is put in the water and pulled.

Open canoe

Holding the open canoe paddle is much simpler. First decide which side to paddle on. For paddling on the right side, hold the grip or handle with your left hand, your fingers resting on top and your thumb curled underneath. The lower hand (right) is held about the same distance apart as with the kayak, a little wider than shoulder width. Use your body as well as your arms to paddle; although this may feel awkward at first, it is less tiring than just using your arms. This description is for paddling on the right.

Keeping both arms nearly straight, twist your body slightly so that your right shoulder is forward of your left. Reaching as far forward as you can without over-stretching, put your paddle in the water, your lower hand slightly more forward. Keep the paddle shaft vertical and, moving your arms as an integral part of your body, bring your body more upright, twisting at the waist so that your shoulders and upper body face as square as possible to the side of the canoe with your left shoulder now forwards. At the same time pull backwards with both hands, keeping both arms relatively straight. Your upper hand (right) should keep roughly at the same height all the way through at about nose height.

When the paddle blade reaches your hips, lift it out of the water and feather it (slice it through the air) to start again. Feathering creates less wind resistance and the blade does not catch the top of waves. This is the recovery phase of the stroke where your upper hand can drop lower to lift the paddle out of the water and prepare for the next stroke.

Mistakes generally made are that the upper hand either drops across in front of the body or drops down towards the water in the stroke. Both of these mean that you are not using the larger groups of body muscles, only your arms.

Getting into and out of canoes

Getting into and out of canoes is the most unstable moment and initially care is needed. You will quickly grasp the idea though with practice. The tricky part is when you are poised halfway between the shore and sitting or kneeling in the boat, where the boat has a tendency to slide away from the bank at inopportune moments if it is not controlled. The first thing is to find the best place to get in – where a straight piece of bank and the boat can be as close together as possible and at about the same height.

Open canoe

An open canoe is easier to get into than a kayak. Make sure that the canoe is fully in the water and put your paddle either in the canoe or on the ground beside it. Keep your body weight as low as you can on the bank, close to the edge. Keep all your weight on the bank and use a hand to support you. Reach across to the canoe with your foot nearest to it and place your foot carefully into the middle of the canoe, where you are going to paddle (if solo then in the centre, if tandem then at one of the ends). Use a seat or thwart near to you to place a hand on in the middle of it to help transfer your weight smoothly and low down into the boat. Do not forget your paddle.

To get out is just the reverse. The technique is to try and pull both the bank and canoe together, rather than let them be pushed apart as you step from one to the other.

Kayak

Getting into a kayak is similar, but you just have to get more of your body into it. There are various ways to get into the water – from an exciting 'slipway' launch sliding down a bank, or getting in and then pushing off the ground with your hands. None of these are good for the bottom of the boat, but are sometimes more convenient.

For the gentlest method on the boat, make sure that the kayak is afloat and still will be when you get in it. Put the paddle down where you will be able to reach it when you are in (I usually put mine across the front of my boat and the shore).

Keep your body weight low, supported by your hands, one on

the bank and the other on the rear of the cockpit rim and put your near foot into the cockpit. Keep your weight on both hands, while you put your other leg in the cockpit. If the cockpit is small, sit with care on the back of the cockpit to slide your legs in, then quickly but carefully sit down.

Likewise, getting out is the reverse. Put the paddle beside the boat on the bank or across the front deck and get your feet as close to your seat as possible. If necessary put both hands on the cockpit rim towards the back so you can sit on it to slide your legs out. Quickly but carefully transfer your weight to the bank one foot at a time keeping your weight low and directly over your feet.

Capsizing and emptying

You do not have to capsize straight away, but knowing what to do in case it happens accidentally is important. I have seen some people believe that their boat is going over and do their best to get out as soon as possible which, on rare occasions, has resulted in them getting wet but the boat staying upright.

Kayak

The method of getting out will vary slightly depending on the size of your cockpit, so I will describe the exit for a smaller cockpit first.

Wait for the kayak to go completely upside down and if you are wearing a spray-deck release it with the release strap. Place your hands by your hips near the cockpit rim, push against it and lift your bottom off the seat. Keep your legs straight, lean forward and imagine that you are taking off a pair of trousers, the kayak being the trousers. The whole process only takes about three seconds, it just seems longer. Two common mistakes often made are instinctive survival responses such as not going completely upside down before getting out and fighting to get some air. Both make getting out more difficult. Capsize is a discipline which becomes smoother and less scary with practice.

6.5 Coming out of your kayak is like taking off a pair of trousers.

If your cockpit is a keyhole cockpit, then you may not need to use your hands to lift your bottom off the seat and getting your legs out will be easier. It is with this type of cockpit that I have seen people throw themselves out of their kayak before it is even over.

Once you are out of your kayak, leave it upside down and swim to one end and hold on to it. You can either swim, taking both the kayak and paddle, to shallow water or the shore to empty your kayak, or wait for someone else from your group to rescue you and empty it for you. When you swim your boat to the shore, the best way is on your back or side, using a steady kick with your legs.

A capsized or swamped canoe can be paddled to shallow water

Do not lift a swamped canoe. Roll it onto its side and allow it to drain, keeping the canoe level

Once the kayak is light enough, see-saw the rest of the water out

If you are on your own, see-saw using the angle of the slope or bank

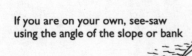

6.6 Emptying boats.

Open canoe

Getting out of an open canoe is easy. If you are paddling with more than one person in the same boat and it capsizes, make sure that all of you are out. If it is upside down then roll it the right way up to make sure. The procedure for swimming to shallow water is the same as for a kayak – go to one end, grab the painter and pull it free if you need to. Using the painter allows you to get yourself to shallow water more quickly and then pull the boat in when you can stand up. Swimming an open canoe the same distance to shore as a kayak will take longer because there is more boat and water to move.

Emptying

Emptying kayaks will be easy as long as there is enough buoyancy fitted. Whatever the boat though, it is best to get to shallow water and turn the boat on its side so that as much water drains out as possible. Let gravity do the work for you. The water will drain out if you lift one end very slowly. As it empties you can gradually lift it higher. To drain a kayak, lift one end and then the other, sea-saw style. There is always some water reluctant to leave the boat so a sponge is useful to get the last drops out.

Emptying swamped open canoes can be done alone but it is always easier with help. Emptying boats in deep water is nearly impossible on your own. Other methods of emptying boats are covered in Chapter 7.

7

Paddling techniques

The strokes

Perfect strokes only come with time and practice, and what may be a good stroke to use in one situation may not be as good in another. The varying sizes and body shapes of people affect the outcome of strokes and we all have differing ranges of strength and flexibility too. What is appropriate for a 12-year-old may not be suitable for an adult and vice versa. So do not worry too much about perfect technique for now, work on safe, comfortable strokes for you.

Range of strokes

The range of strokes that you need will depend on the design of the boat that you are using. Boats that turn easily need a lot of control to go straight and offer exciting possibilities for later. Boats that are straight-running (used for long distances on lakes or canals) do not need a great range of strokes to keep them straight so you do not need to know as many.

Places to learn

The place you choose to learn these strokes for the first time should be made carefully. The water should be sheltered from the wind as much as possible and not be moving, or only moving slowly. Such places could be canals, lakes, still rivers or very sheltered bays or inlets of the sea.

There should be no chance of you being swept out of your area by wind or current. Spend time finding the right place. It will be safer and easier to learn.

Paddling forwards
Going in a straight line

The most frustrating part of learning to canoe is getting the boat to do what you want it to do, when you want it to happen. After spending a few months paddling in a sea kayak, I had difficulty getting a general purpose kayak to go in a straight line. I felt as though I was having to learn all over again; no one was more embarrassed than I was. Rest assured that the straight line will come with patience and practice. Be tolerant with yourself as you go through this learning process.

The secret is not to fight against the boat too hard and not to do anything too suddenly or violently. Paddle gently but firmly using your paddles as you would use your arms, if you were swimming. Arms in swimming and paddles in canoeing are placed in front of you as far as you can comfortably reach, grip the water and pull you forwards, and leave the water ready for the next stroke, at almost right-angles to your body. The movement is as smooth, continuous and as rhythmic as possible, and requires rotation of the body for each stroke and extension of the arms, neither of which needs to be excessively thought about in the early stages.

So let it all happen as naturally as possible, working on efficiency and technique later.

Why will my canoe not go straight?

There are many reasons why a canoe will not go in a straight line: the pull with the paddle on each side may be unequal, or the blade on one side may be slicing through the water instead of gripping it. Your position on the seat will affect the canoe's pivot point; the distance your hands are apart on the paddle will affect the leverage applied to each stroke (are they the same distance from each end of the blade?) and so on.

Even when paddling correctly the canoe actually moves in a zig-zag fashion, so here are some general guide-lines on moving in a straight line.

Going in a straight line

- Make sure that you sit upright and in the centre of your seat.

- Check that your hands grip the paddle the same distance from each blade and are just over shoulder width apart.

- Keep your kayak moving, but at a slow speed.

- Line up the nose of your kayak with something on the shore as a target to aim at, so that you know when you go off course.

- As soon as the kayak moves slightly off course, just paddle on one side to correct it, then go back to alternating sides when you are back on course.

- Imagine putting your paddle into quick-setting concrete which fixes the blade in place. Then pull the kayak towards the paddle as if the kayak was resting on marbles. This is what happens on the water. The paddle in the water provides resistance for you to pull your kayak along. If you find this hard to believe and think that you pull the paddle past you, try the same thing in the air and see if you move anywhere. Without sufficient resistance to move you towards the paddle you will just stay still.

Paddling the kayak
What to do if you go off course

When your kayak goes off course, the problem more than likely is that the back end has skidded off line, a bit like a rear end skid or handbrake turn in a car. So it is towards the back of the kayak that you need to make the corrections.

Two effective ways that you can do this are: a sweep stroke on the move, or a stern rudder. These strokes will allow you to keep your forward momentum and not slow you down too much.

Sweep stroke

This stroke is part of the stationary sweep stroke used to spin the kayak. In a stationary sweep stroke the paddle blade is kept just below the surface, but fully immersed to get maximum grip and

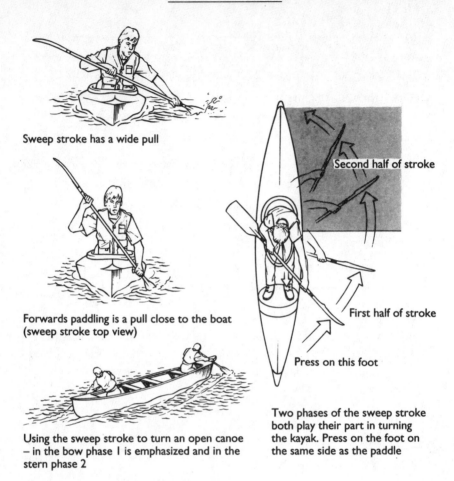

Sweep stroke has a wide pull

Forwards paddling is a pull close to the boat
(sweep stroke top view)

Using the sweep stroke to turn an open canoe
– in the bow phase I is emphasized and in the
stern phase 2

Second half of stroke

First half of stroke

Press on this foot

Two phases of the sweep stroke
both play their part in turning
the kayak. Press on the foot on
the same side as the paddle

7.1 The sweep stroke.

resistance from the water. The paddle travels in a wide arc from
the very front of the kayak to the very back. The part of this
stroke that will help you to keep straight is the back half because
it is the rear of the kayak that is skidding off course. The skid will
be brought under control if the paddle is swept in a wide arc,
starting opposite your hips and finishing at the very back of the
kayak. As well as the paddle moving in this arc, your shoulders
need to follow the same line for the stroke to be fully effective.
To get the feel of this body twist, or rotation, hold the paddle in

your normal paddling position in front of you. While keeping the paddle in the air just above your boat and with your arms almost straight, twist gently sideways at your waist until the paddle and your shoulders are parallel with the length of the kayak (or as near to this position as you can get). Do this a few times, twisting from one side to the other to feel what it is like. You will also find it easier if, at the same time, you push with your feet on the footrest. Push with the right foot when twisting to the right and with the left foot when twisting to the left.

Do this again, but this time with the paddle in the water. The whole blade should be just below the water's surface. Start as far forward as you can, close to the bow and reaching out in a long, wide arc from the side of the kayak, sweep the paddle all the way round, as far back as you can, finishing close to the stern. When the paddle reaches the stern, lift it out of the water ready to do another sweep. Repeat this on the same side a few times, turning the kayak in circles, then change sides. This is the stationary sweep stroke.

Sweep stroke on the move

The part of the stationary sweep stroke that you need to keep yourself in a straight line is the second half. Dividing the stroke into two, the front half starts at the bow and does a wide sweep as far as your hips. The second half starts at your hips and does a wide sweep to the stern.

Keep the kayak moving slowly and, as soon as it skids off course, do the back half of the sweep stroke. To help twist your body as far round as you can, try looking at the blade as it goes round. Keep the arm doing the wide sweep with the paddle reasonably straight and try and touch the back of the kayak at the end of the stroke. Exaggerating the movement will help you to know when you have gone as far as you can.

To begin with, do not be tempted to do the stroke too fast. It may also take a couple of these strokes to bring the boat back on course. Make sure that you are using an object on the shore to help you gauge when the kayak is moving on and off your straight line.

Stern rudder

This stroke is a steering stroke and only works while the boat is moving forwards. Without changing your grip on the paddle, turn slightly sideways and put the paddle in the water at the stern of the boat. The rear blade trails behind, completely submerged in the water, close to the side of the kayak and should be upright like a ship's rudder.

You can now steer your kayak. The side of the kayak on which you put your paddle into the water, is the side that you will turn towards. Putting your paddle in the water on the right means that you can turn to the right. Practice doing this on both sides

The trailing blade is submerged but upright, like a ship's rudder

By pushing the paddle further away, the kayak will turn right, and by pulling the paddle towards you, it will turn more to the left

7.2 The stern rudder.

picking up some speed gently and, as soon as you skid off course, use the stern rudder to bring yourself back in line with the target on the shore.

For fine tuning of the stern rudder, try and combine it with forward paddling to keep up your speed. Then try changing the direction of pressure that you apply to the blade when it is in the water. Put your paddle in the water on the right and when you push the blade slightly away from the kayak, you will turn further to the right. If you keep it straight, you will go straight and if you pull the blade towards the boat, you will turn to the left. Now you have the option to steer somewhat in both directions, without having to change sides. The same principle applies when you use your paddle on the left.

Paddling the open canoe

Open canoes can be paddled solo or tandem. If paddled tandem they are easier to learn to control than kayaks in the initial stages. Two people can get into an open canoe and very quickly become competent with the necessary manoeuvring, which is why they are so popular for one-off canoe sessions. However there is a lot more finesse to this aspect of the sport than you might at first appreciate in a one-off session. Paddling solo requires more skill to provide both the power to move and control for the steering, especially as this is generally done just on one side.

Paddling position

The position you place yourself in will depend on several things such as the size of the boat, whether you are paddling solo or tandem and the amount of wind affecting the steering. What is important to remember though is that at no point in any stroke do you lean your body outside of the gunwales as this just increases your instability. Your body weight should always be along the centre line of the boat and either be upright or leaning backwards or slightly forwards. When the boat leans sideways, your body pivots at your hips to keep upright.

For greater stability in waves, wind and white water, it is better to kneel. Kneeling lowers your centre of gravity and reduces your chance of capsizing. Kneel with your bottom resting against the front edge of your seat and your knees spread apart as far as possible. This kneeling position also allows you to put more power into your strokes.

Trim

The open canoe sits high off the water and in windy conditions it gets blown off course easily and becomes difficult to steer. Adjusting your paddling position in the canoe for the conditions in relation to the bow and stern is called trim. Imagine a weather vane on a windy day, as this is how your canoe will respond in the wind. The wind will blow the higher end around. If you are paddling into the wind then put more weight in the bow by using equipment or moving your paddling position forward or, in tandem boats, the heavier person could go in the bow. The same applies for paddling downwind: put the weight nearest the wind in the stern. If you are travelling across the wind solo, let the wind blow the bow towards your paddling side. Paddling tandem, the stern paddler generally overrides the bow but there are more variables, so experiment with which side the bow and stern should be paddled on to go most easily in the straightest line.

Going in a straight line

All the references to paddling in a straight line and skidding for kayaks, apply to open canoes as well. The sweep stroke on the move is also very relevant, particularly paddling tandem for the person in the stern. The goon stroke and J-stroke in open canoes work in the same way as the stern rudder in kayaks, but are slightly different in their mechanics.

Paddling tandem

When paddling tandem in an open canoe, paddle on opposite sides of the canoe to each other in a synchronized manner for better balance and to help the canoe travel in a straight line. The person in the bow generally provides the power and fine tunes the steering, whereas the person in the stern provides some power and most of the steering. Both paddlers should switch sides occasionally when paddling to reduce muscle fatigue, and also change positions from bow to stern to gain experience in the other position and an understanding of your partner's job.

Paddling solo

The solo paddling position can be even more varied than tandem for the same reasons mentioned earlier. A central position in a large boat will be described first and, if you were at all super-stitious about which way your canoe was facing when you tied it down on the roof-rack, then you may want to think about (not) paddling solo in large open canoes, because it is better to paddle them backwards!

Position yourself in front of the centre thwart or portage yoke, where you will have a thwart for kneeling against in the same way as described for paddling tandem. However, you should not sit on this thwart because it will probably break. You can also position yourself behind the centre thwart but either way the canoe is very wide at its centre, so kneel to one side of the boat to be able to put your paddle comfortably in the water as this will lean the canoe towards that side. If you wish to sit on a seat to change your position, then sit on the bow seat the wrong way round facing the stern. The seat this way round is as close as you can get to the centre of the boat and still sit down.

While sitting on the seat, keep your knee below the gunwale otherwise you will need to lift your paddle over it during the strokes. I prefer to wedge my knee under the gunwale on the side that I am paddling to give me more purchase. Kneeling is a pos-ition that takes time to get used to, but can be made more com-fortable by resting on closed-cell foam put on the bottom of the boat which will also stop you sliding around as much. You can use closed-cell foam to make knee pads.

J-stroke

This is the main stroke which allows you to paddle on one side and provide both power for movement and steering for direction. To do the J-stroke requires a very flexible wrist. It is a forward stroke with a turning stroke added at the end. When paddling tandem, the J-stroke is done by the person in the stern.

Start the J-stroke by doing a forward stroke and when the blade reaches your hips, instead of taking the blade out of the water, hold the handle firmly and turn the thumb of your top hand downwards towards the water. This will roll the blade through a right-angle and turn it parallel to the side of the canoe.

When the blade is parallel to the side of the canoe, pry or push it away from the boat. This forces the stern to move away from the paddle side. You can make the pry phase of the J-stroke easier in the early stages if you use the gunwale as a lever to push the boat away. Remember to keep your fingers out of the way if you do this.

Goon stroke

The goon stroke has been so nicknamed because of its inefficiency as a stroke. However, it has the same effect as the J-stroke and the stern rudder in a kayak, but it does not need a flexible wrist like the J-stroke. The goon stroke is a forward paddle stroke at the end of which the thumb on your top hand is turned upwards, the opposite way to a J-stroke. The blade is then pushed away from the canoe to steer. The goon stroke is easier to do than the J-stroke and is used a lot in white water, but it causes more drag which slows you down.

Stopping and turning
Kayak and open canoe

Canoes do not have brakes so to stop, just paddle in the opposite direction from the one in which you are moving. If you are paddling forwards and you want to stop, just paddle backwards using the back of the blade and vice versa. Do a series of quick, shallow

The J-stroke – turn the thumb on your top hand downwards and pry the paddle away for the steering phase

The goon stroke – turn the thumb on your top hand upwards for the steering phase and pry away from the side of the canoe

7.3 The J-stroke and the goon stroke.

reverse strokes with only part of the blade immersed in the water. This will stop you in as straight a line as possible, gradually applying the brakes rather than violently locking them up, which could possibly result in a broken paddle blade, a capsize, or an injury.

Paddling backwards

This is the same as paddling forwards except that the back of the blade is used for the stroke. The main difference, however, is that the body has to twist more, both to perform the strokes and to look where you are going.

In an open canoe, to paddle backwards in a straight line, the stern person provides the power and the bow person does the steering using draw strokes, prys or reverse J-strokes.

Reverse sweep stroke

Again this is the same as the forward sweep stroke but the paddle just starts at the stern. All the mechanics are the same. Make a wide, shallow arc starting at the stern and sweep the paddle forwards finishing at the bow.

Combining sweep strokes
Kayak

Combining forward and reverse sweep strokes will turn the kayak in a full circle. To turn to the left, do a forward sweep stroke on the right then reach behind you to the stern on the left and do a backwards sweep stroke. Practice doing continuous forward and reverse sweep strokes to see how few strokes it can take you to turn in a complete circle. Do not forget to practise sweep strokes in both directions.

Open canoes

The principle is the same as in a kayak except that to turn in a complete circle paddling tandem, both forward and reverse sweep strokes need to be performed at the same time. To turn to the right, the stern paddler (paddling on the left) does a forward sweep stroke and the bow paddler (paddling on the right) does a reverse sweep stroke. A more efficient method for turning tandem open canoes in a circle is for both paddlers to do draw strokes which are covered below.

Moving sideways

There are not many other vessels that find it as easy to move sideways as canoes do. The stroke which makes moving sideways possible is called the draw stroke, and the movement over the water is called side-slip.

For both kayaks and tandem open canoes this stroke is the same, but the movement of the boats is different. In a kayak and solo open canoe with just one person doing the draw stroke, the boat will move sideways, but when paddling tandem in an open canoe both paddlers do draw strokes on their respective sides, and the boat turns very effectively in a circle. This is a more effective way of turning in a circle than using sweep strokes.

Draw stroke

Hold your hands in their normal paddling position, twist your upper body sideways, reach as far away from the boat level with your hip as is comfortable, and put the paddle in the water as near vertical as possible by stretching your upper arm.

The lower blade should be completely submerged, deep in the water, square to your hip and parallel to the side of the boat. In a kayak your top arm is positioned across your head. In an open canoe your top hand is level with your forehead and your elbow is bent and close to your body, pointing downwards. Keep your forearm as parallel to the paddle shaft as possible. Your elbow position is especially important for paddling in shallow water or white water in case you hit a rock with your paddle while doing a draw stroke. Your arm will then be in a stable position and have a chance to move upwards, doing as much as is possible to prevent shoulder dislocation.

With your paddle in position and keeping the boat level, gently pull the canoe towards the paddle but be careful with the next stage so you do not 'trip' the canoe up. Before the paddle and the canoe come together, the blade must be recovered for the next stroke, either underwater or through the air. To do an underwater recovery, keep the blade submerged while you turn it at right-angles to the side of the boat and slice it away from you. It is the edge of the blade facing the back of the boat that leads the blade away from you. (In an open canoe turn the thumb on your top hand away from you.) You must turn the blade completely, before the blade and canoe meet, and before you attempt to slice it back out, otherwise you will 'trip' the canoe up over the paddle.

To recover the blade out of the water, the movement is the same, but the paddle blade is sliced upwards and out, before you reach over the water away from the boat again. Another out of the water recovery is to slice the blade out backwards, towards the stern, before repeating the movement.

You can vary the sideways direction in which you move your boat by starting the pull more towards the bow or stern. Pull more towards the bow to move sideways and forwards, or more towards the stern to move sideways and backwards. Other variations also exist which you will no doubt discover with practice when you move away from and towards other boats.

The cross-bow draw (open canoe)

The cross-bow draw is the same as the bow draw except that it is only performed by the bow paddler and it is done on the non-paddle side. To do this stroke you need to twist your body sideways as much as possible to face the paddle on the opposite side of the canoe. Almost the same grip is kept with both hands throughout the transfer from one side to the other. As you change sides over the bow, turn your thumb on the top hand to face forwards before putting the paddle in the water, and still keep your elbow pointing downwards.

The pry (open canoe)

In order for a tandem open canoe to side-slip (move sideways), one person will need to do a draw stroke, as above, and the other will need to do a pry. The pry is the reverse of a draw stroke and pushes the boat away from the paddle side. The pry is a more powerful stroke than the draw stroke, as it uses the gunwale and bilge for leverage.

Turn your body sideways as for the draw stroke. Put the paddle in the water right next to the canoe, opposite your hips. The

The draw stroke   **The cross-bow draw**

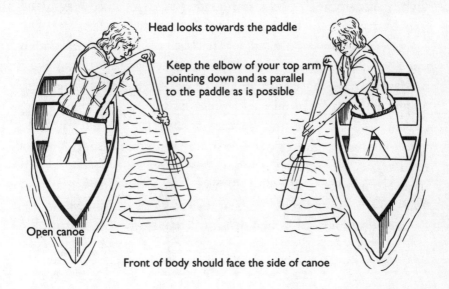

Head looks towards the paddle

Keep the elbow of your top arm pointing down and as parallel to the paddle as is possible

Open canoe

Front of body should face the side of canoe

The draw stroke

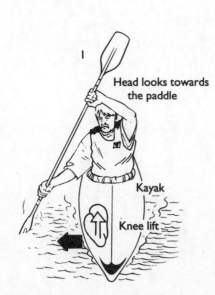

I

Head looks towards the paddle

Kayak

Knee lift

2

Keep the blade deep and the boat level and your top hand across your head

7.4 The draw stroke and the cross-bow draw.

blade is deep in the water, parallel to the side of the canoe and slightly underneath it. Your top hand is at about nose height and leaning away from the canoe, but letting the paddle shaft rest against the gunwale and bilge. The heel of your lower hand is just above, or resting on, the gunwale and loosely holding the paddle, but keeping it firmly in place. Be careful not to trap your fingers between the paddle and gunwale.

Using the gunwale and bilge as a lever for the paddle shaft, pull your top arm towards your nose, across your body, but not too far past the vertical position. If you pull the paddle too far across your body, you will pull the gunwale down and lift water upwards which will rock the boat instead of moving it sideways.

Turn the thumb of your top hand away from you, to turn the

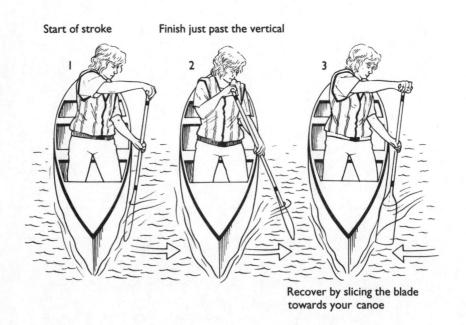

7.5 The pry.

blade through 90 degrees, ready to slice the blade back towards you and under the canoe slightly. The pry is a very short and powerful stroke rather than a long slow one.

Keeping upright – recovery strokes

A recovery stroke uses the surface of the water as a lever for a short period of time, in order for the paddler to regain the canoe's normal upright position. A brace uses the same recovery stroke, but is no longer a recovery stroke when regaining balance is prolonged and support is gained for more than an instant. Recovering from an off-balance position could take a second or so, or it could take longer. The difference between using a recovery stroke or a brace on occasions can, therefore, be quite subtle. However, use of the brace is more likely to arise in rough water, such as surfing on a wave, when the moving water provides a mobile platform which gives support.

Trying to stay upright is instinctive. When beginners realize that they are losing their balance, they often let go of the paddle and try to use their hands to remain upright. The effective recovery stroke therefore, is this instinctive reaction with the hands, converted to use with the paddles to prevent the canoe from tipping over.

You are stable in a canoe when your centre of gravity is above that of the boat. Once your centre of gravity is offset from the canoe's centre of gravity, you will capsize unless you use the paddle to lean on temporarily while you bring the boat back upright.

Practise this balance control by gently rocking the boat from side to side. This will be easier in a kayak as you can grip with your knees, but unless you have thigh straps in an open canoe it will be more difficult, especially if you are in a large open canoe on your own. Tandem is easier as you have a smaller space in which to slide about.

While gently rocking the boat you will probably have found that it is quite easy to stay upright. This is because you will have instinctively pivoted at your hips and kept your centre of gravity over the canoe's centre of gravity. If you now slow this rocking action down, you will be able to place the canoe more onto one of its sides, or edges. When the canoe is on its edge, a flick upwards with the lower knee (the one you are leaning towards) will bring the canoe back to a level position. Try and balance the canoe on its edge for a second and then repeat this manoeuvre on the other side.

Low-brace recovery stroke
Kayak

Lean the kayak on to its edge and reach out as far as you can with your arm and paddle on the side that the kayak is tipping towards. Keep the paddle as horizontal as is comfortable, with the back of the blade on the water and make sure that it is flat, like your hand would be. You will find that the paddle is now below your wrist and elbows, so keep them in this position above the paddle when you do the low brace recovery stroke.

When you reach out with your paddle to support yourself use the blade to provide enough resistance on top of the the water to flick your lower knee upwards and bring the boat back to a level position. The blade will only stay on the surface for a short time as it sinks a little as you push off it, so you need to be careful when you lift it out. A good way of lifting the blade is to lower your elbows and roll your wrist and knuckles backwards and upwards until you can slice the blade upwards and out.

Open canoe

The principle is the same as with the kayak and the stroke very similar. As the boat leans over, reach out as far as you can with your hands, keeping your knuckles down and elbows up, but remember not to lean your body outside of the gunwales. Make sure that your top hand is as low as possible next to the gunwale and that your body is either upright or leaning backwards as you drive off your paddle. If you paddle tandem, the low-brace is

Open canoe

Kayak

Think of the paddle as an extension of your hand

7.6 Low-brace recovery stoke.

done when the boat tips towards your paddle side. Your partner does a high-brace on his or her paddle side, which is in fact a draw stroke done very quickly.

High-brace recovery stroke
Kayak

The high-brace recovery stroke is used when the body is well off balance, allowing the paddler to get his or her boat back upright from what seems like an incredibly off balance position. At these times the low-brace is of little use because the body position required by the low brace is too upright. Good knee and hip flicks are the key to doing the high recovery stroke well and also put much less of a load on the paddle. The footrest comes into more use too, giving you greater purchase on the inside of the kayak.

The high-brace stroke can be compared to hanging from a bar, part way through doing a pull up, with the palm of your hands facing away from you. This stroke uses the drive face of the blade as opposed to the back face of the blade in the low-brace. This time the paddle shaft is above your wrists and elbows but below your head and as horizontal as possible. Keeping your paddle below head height is important. If your paddle moves above head height then your shoulders have less room to 'give' if leverage is applied. If much force is applied with your paddle while it is held above your head, then shoulder dislocation is more likely as this is a less stable position for your shoulder joint.

In preparation for a high-brace on the right side, hold your paddle in the normal paddling position at shoulder height, with the drive face of the right blade facing the water (downwards).

Tip the kayak over to the right and eventually the blade will hit

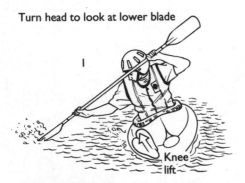

Turn head to look at lower blade

Keep your hands and paddle below head height. The timing between hitting the water and applying knee lift needs much practice

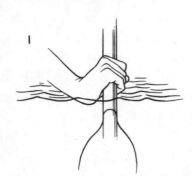

To recover the blade from the water after it has sunk, roll your wrists and knuckles and slice it out

7.7 high-brace recovery stroke.

the surface of the water. Do not be tempted to put the blade in too soon. As soon as the blade hits the water, flick the kayak back upright using a good knee and hip flick, at the same time as briefly pulling down on the paddle shaft. Keep your body weight as low as possible and try not to lift your head out too early. Then bring your body upright and back into balance.

To recover the blade out of the water (it will sink in the same way as in the low brace recovery stroke) roll your wrist and knuckles again, but this time roll them forwards and downwards lifting your elbows up, to slice the blade upwards and out.

Open canoe

As mentioned earlier, the high-brace is done when the canoe tips away from your paddling side. It is in effect a draw stroke and feels as though you are grabbing for water to pull yourself upright. An important aspect of this stroke is being able to react quickly and put your hips in the best position to help balance the canoe. Put your hips where you want the canoe to be which, when using a high-brace, will be on the high side of the canoe as you want the canoe to be level. It is also possible to do a pry instead of a high-brace. A pry will have the same effect in keeping the canoe upright and allow you to use the gunwale as a pivot if need be, but you still need to get your hips on the high side of the canoe.

Other turning and steering strokes

The next two strokes, low-brace turn and bow rudder, are a different kind of turning and steering stroke. They are applied once the turning movement has been started. They do not initiate the turning movement as in the sweep stroke or stern rudder.

Edging and leaning

These two terms, edging and leaning, are two different things and are important for you to understand for both the low-brace turn and, further on in this book, for paddling in white water.

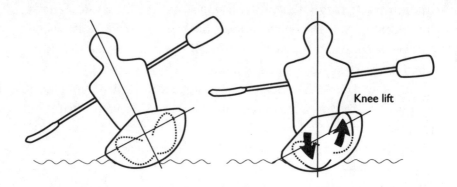

Leaning is like cornering on a
bicycle, moving your body weight

Knee lift

Edging is like sitting on half of your
bottom and keeping your body upright

7.8 Edging and leaning.

Edging is what you do to the canoe. Tilt the canoe slightly on to its side (its edge) by lifting with your knee and thigh on one side, a bit like sitting on half of your bottom. To put the canoe on to its right edge, lift your left knee and thigh. You can still keep your balance by pivoting at your hips and sitting upright.

Leaning is what you do with your upper body. Lean your upper body sideways, off its normal centre of gravity, as if you are cornering on a bicycle.

Low-brace turn (kayak and open canoe)

The object of the low-brace turn is to make the canoe turn and still keep its forward speed. The low-brace turn is a very stable stroke and it is important in white water.

The position of the paddle is virtually the same as for the low-brace recovery stroke except that, as the canoe is moving forwards, the front edge of the blade needs to be lifted slightly so that it skids across the surface with you and does not dive into the water and 'trip' you up.

With the low-brace turn it is important that the canoe is edged. This reduces the surface area of the boat in contact with the water making the turn easier and more efficient. In an open canoe, however, edging well is tricky without thigh straps to hold you in place as it is heavier to move. Without thigh straps, your body needs to be more towards one side or, what I prefer to do as well, is wedge my knee under the higher gunwale to help hold the tilt and keep me in balance. Edging is important in moving or white water.

To do a low-brace turn, first get the canoe moving, decide which way you want to turn, then edge the canoe on that side. To turn right, edge on the right and, at the same time, put the paddle blade flat on the surface, with the front edge of the blade lifted slightly. It is important not to lean too heavily on the paddle blade, just shift your point of balance and the combination

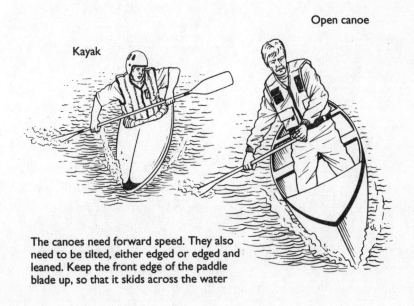

Open canoe

Kayak

The canoes need forward speed. They also need to be tilted, either edged or edged and leaned. Keep the front edge of the paddle blade up, so that it skids across the water

7.9 The low-brace turn.

of edging the canoe and the drag of the blade will create a smooth and steady turn. How much you lean or if you need to lean, will depend on how tight you need to turn, exactly the same as cornering on a bicycle. To help initiate the turn of the low-brace, do a forward sweep stroke on the opposite side to which you will turn. As soon as the nose of the canoe starts to turn, start the tilt. When the turn is finished, or the canoe slows down, simply sit upright. Or, if you are ready to paddle, just skid the blade forwards over the water and start your stroke.

Low-brace turn (open canoe, tandem)
Again the principle is the same in a tandem open canoe. When paddling tandem, however, only one person needs to do the low-brace turn, the other person can help keep the canoe on its edge.

The bow rudder (kayak)
The bow rudder is a very dynamic, attacking stroke composed of many subtle paddle movements found in all of the other strokes – pushes, pulls, slices and so on. These variations can make the boat spin quickly, slow it down, speed it up, carve a slow turn or make it change direction. It is an ideal stroke for moving water. The power in the stroke comes from the position of your body, which is twisted to the side and coiled a bit like a spring. To get the paddle into position and the blade at a good angle, requires a flexible body, arms and wrists. When it is in position, the paddle is used as a pivot to steer the boat around.

The position of the paddle is very similar to that of the draw stroke. The paddle should be angled forwards, not far off vertical, and placed slightly forward of your body and away from the side of the kayak, keeping the lower blade well immersed. Your body needs to twist to one side, keeping your upper arm across the top of your forehead. The lower blade is at an open angle, which means that you have opened up the 'throttle' and rolled your wrist and knuckles backwards, to make the blade form a V with the side of the boat.

Front view   Top view

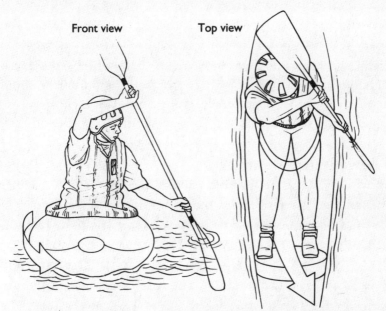

Look at lower paddle blade   Push with the knee and foot on the side
opposite to the paddle to help drive the kayak
round the turn

7.10 The bow rudder.

The bow rudder is usually used when the kayak has already
started to turn. In flat water the canoe first needs some forward
speed, then the turn is initiated by a forward sweep stroke on the
side opposite to the way you want to turn. Sweep on the right,
bow rudder on the left.

After the sweep stroke on the right, twist your body to the left,
open the blade and plant it in the water, level with your knee but
away from the side of the boat. The narrower the V the finer the
turn; the wider the V the more the blade will catch the water and
the greater the braking affect will be, which also makes the
paddle more difficult to hold in place. Try linking the bow rudder
with a forward stroke. After the turn, roll your wrist and knuckles

forwards, closing the 'throttle' (which turns the blade inwards) and then pull it straight through.

The bow rudder can be linked with many strokes. Even in its simplest from it requires much practice and, on flat water, it is difficult to simulate the exact movements that will be experienced on moving water. It is also a stroke that you should not be timid with, or it will be difficult to do. Use it positively, with purpose and practice it often. It is the most versatile of strokes.

The bow cut (open canoe)

The bow cut is used by the solo paddler and by the bow paddler when paddling tandem. It is the same as the bow rudder in kayaks and likewise the same principles apply. Your body is twisted sideways. The paddle is held in the same position, as far forward as you can comfortably reach, not far off the vertical and away from the side of the canoe. The top hand is across the top of your forehead and your elbow is as low as possible. The

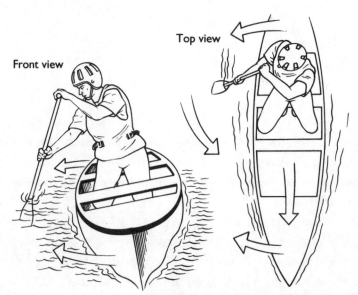

Top view

Front view

Twist your body sideways and have your top hand no higher than your head

7.11 The bow cut.

thumb on your top hand is turned towards you which opens the blade into a V with the side of the boat. When the water catches the blade the canoe is drawn to the paddle side.

Your top hand should not be higher than your head for the same reasons as given in the open canoe draw stroke and the high brace recovery stroke in kayaks. The position that your shoulder presents above your head height is a less stable position for the joint, and dislocation is more likely if you hit something with the paddle in shallow or moving water.

The cross-bow cut (open canoe)

The stroke is the same as the bow cut, but on the non-paddle side of the canoe. Keep almost the same grip on the paddle with your upper hand and allow your lower hand to slide round the shaft a little to be more comfortable. Lift the paddle over the bow, the thumb on your top hand forwards and away from you, so that the blade is rotated through 180 degrees and place it in the water, in the same position as you would use on your paddle side. To prevent shoulder dislocation in shallow or moving water, keep your elbow pointing downwards and forwards along the paddle shaft as far as is comfortable. Your upper body needs to be flexible for this stroke.

The eskimo roll (kayaks)

The Eskimo roll is the technique used for righting a kayak after a capsize. There are many variations and types of roll and not all of them can be covered here. It is not essential to learn to roll, but for some disciplines of the sport, such as sea kayaking, surfing and white water, it is an important skill to learn for safety.

It is easier to learn to roll with someone else who will be able to see what you are doing and so you can both take turns to rest in between your attempts. The movements for rolling are not difficult, but they do require some flexibility. What usually takes time to sort out is the sequence of movements and the inevitable disorientation as a result of being upside down. The best way to learn the movements at first is kinaesthetically, which is feeling the movements through your body until you can repeat them unconsciously. The movements are difficult to think through initially, so just doing them without thinking too much about what should happen is sometimes easier.

The best place to learn the mechanics of rolling is in a swimming pool where it is warmer and more comfortable. The first aspect of rolling is all about being comfortable upside down in the boat, which is achieved through lots of fun, games, capsizes and anything else which will increase your confidence.

Wearing the minimal amount of canoe clothing is easier in the early stages. If you have a pair of goggles or a mask, this will help you to see what the paddle is doing and if you do not like lots of water up your nose, then a nose clip is a good investment.

Hip flick

A good hip flick is the key to effortless rolling. The principle of the hip flick is to right the boat far enough so that the force of the boat's natural buoyancy will help with the rest of the righting, while your body is still in the water. This also allows as little strain as possible on your shoulders. However, leaving your body in the water while you try and right the boat goes against your natural instinct of survival, which is to bring your head to the surface as quickly as possible to breathe. Lots of practice will help you relax your urge to breathe so soon after capsizing.

There are many progressions and exercises which help you to learn the hip flick, but what is useful to do first is to experience the whole range of motions that are possible in a kayak while you are upside down. This will help you to feel what your body is doing. The first attempt I had found me totally confused about what 'up' really meant. When I was told to push my hands up to the surface, instinctively I reached above my head, after all that was up wasn't it? Being upside down meant that I was aiming at the bottom of the pool. Movements such as swinging your body from side to side and front to back, reaching as high out of the

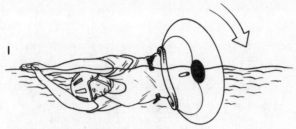

Pull the boat up to this position slowly and
then quickly flick it over

Leave the head and shoulders
in the water until last

7.12 The hip flick.

water as you can or as far down as possible and so on, all help
you discover what range of mobility you really have.

To practise the hip flick and rolling, the kayak needs a footrest
and a spray-deck. The footrest gives you something to push
against to help wedge yourself in the boat. Some beginners find it
hard to 'lock' themselves in even if the kayak fits them well.

The hip and body movement for keeping your balance,
decribed on pages 96-7 is the same action for rolling done under
water. Practise the same side-to-side rocking motion when upside
down in your kayak. To begin working on getting back upright
using the hip flick, hold the side of the pool rail or bar, next to
you and lower the shoulder nearest to it slowly into the water.
Keep the boat close to the bar and your head just above the
water. Try flicking the boat upright using the hip flick, driving
your knee upwards on the same side. Then try this with your
head under water. Once you have flicked the boat up as far as

possible leave your body relaxed in the water. Work on initiating the first move.

Once you are familiar with the hip flick, get your body out of the water by twisting at your waist, leaving your head and shoulders in the water until last. Your hip leaves the water first, then your waist, side, shoulder and head. As you come up, your body is almost lying backwards (depending on the flexibility of your back) along the rear deck of your kayak.

Progress from using both hands to flick up with, to just using your rear hand as this will be a good test of your technique. Practice rolling through 360 degrees by capsizing away from the pool side, finding the bar and flicking yourself back up. If you get your partner to hold a paddle as if it was the bar, they can tell you how much weight you are really putting on it; the less weight you put on the paddle the better your hip flick.

Introducing the paddle

If your hip flick is good you could probably roll up with anything that will give your hands some purchase, such as a swimming float, part of a paddle, or your partner's hands. It is also possible to roll just using your hands on the surface.

Use a paddle and practice the last half of the roll which uses the same technique as the high recovery stroke. Do some recovery strokes with your body completely in the water. As the blade hits the water, flick your hip, leave your body in the water and lie as far back as you can, bringing your shoulders and head up last. Try this with your partner supporting the end of the blade in the water with you completely upside down. When the last part of the roll is familiar, move onto the beginning.

The start of the roll is important because it sets up the position for the whole roll. When you roll in a river or the sea you are unlikely to see what you are doing, so the set-up is done purely by feel. It is worth spending time getting the set-up position right because when you roll for real the set-up position is crucial to the roll's ultimate success.

There are many different types of rolls all based on variations of a few basic techniques and, as with all strokes, people's physique, flexibility and strength will affect which roll suits them best. So do not despair if one roll does not work for you, try another. The two rolls covered here are the screw roll and the pawlata.

The screw roll

The screw roll is the most commonly used roll as the hands remain on the shaft of the paddle in their normal paddling position throughout. The paddle is used as a shorter lever to right the kayak than with the pawlata. The screw roll requires good hip flick and paddle techniques. It is probably a more suitable roll to learn first, particularly for young people and those who have a slight build. For convenience the roll is described for a right-handed paddler. The control hand and control blade referred to are on the right side as for a right-handed paddler.

Hold the paddle in the normal paddling position, your knuckles lined up with the edge of the vertical blade. Lay the paddle alongside you on the left side of the kayak with the back of the control blade flat (horizontal) with the front deck of the kayak. Your left hand (non-control hand) is by your hip. Lean your body well forward, with your front arm also reaching forward. Slide the paddle and both hands off the deck onto the surface of the water on your left side. This is your starting position when you are upside down.

From the starting position upside down, push your hands well towards the surface, into the air, so that the paddle blades will clear the bottom of the boat and not get caught. Your face is close to the deck at this stage and therefore protected in shallow or moving water. Regardless of your paddle position when you capsize you must return to the start position before beginning your roll.

When you are in the start position get your partner to confirm that the blade is on the surface, then push/pull the front blade to

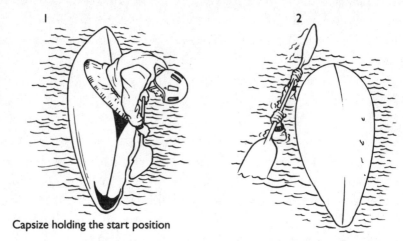

Capsize holding the start position

Reach for the surface. Make sure the paddles are above the surface before sweeping the paddle away from the bow

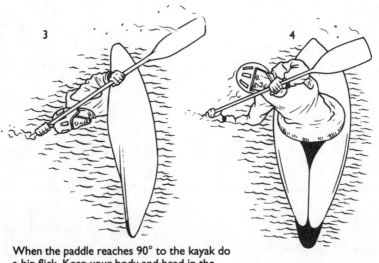

When the paddle reaches 90° to the kayak do a hip flick. Keep your body and head in the water until the last minute

When the boat is level your body will follow

7.13 The screw roll.

your left with a sweeping motion round to 90 degrees to the kayak. Follow the movement of the paddle with your upper body, but do not try to lift your body out of the water. When the paddle reaches 90 degrees, apply your hip flick and continue moving the paddle in the same direction. Your body will be lifted out of the water as the kayak becomes upright. You are now upright.

If you find the initial movement of the paddle awkward from the start position, your partner can begin the movement for you and guide your paddle. To help you in this way, your partner stands at the bow, if necessary holding the kayak and blade together during the capsize. Get yourself into the start position. Your partner then pushes the kayak's bow away from your paddle to start the movement and, if needed, supports the paddle sweep for you.

If you have difficulties:

- Give yourself time to work out the starting position.
- Check the paddle position both above the surface and at 90 degrees.
- Wearing goggles or a mask helps you check the above.
- Do not forget your hip flick.
- Do not try and lift your body out of the water – it will come upright with the kayak.
- Get someone to watch to see what you cannot see.
- The timing of everything is important.
- Take plenty of rests.
- Go back to the point where you were achieving success and work from there. You can increase the paddle leverage by sliding your hands along the shaft closer to the non-control blade.

The pawlata

The pawlata is more forgiving of poor hip flick and paddle techniques and the paddle is used as a longer lever to right the kayak

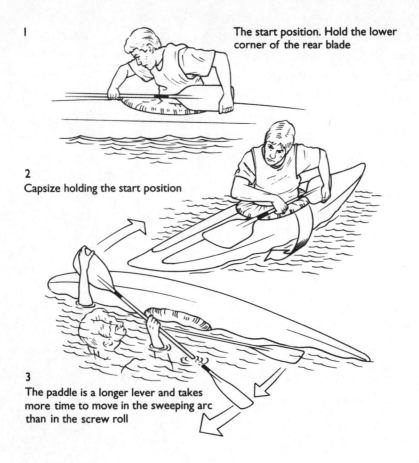

1

The start position. Hold the lower
corner of the rear blade

2

Capsize holding the start position

3

The paddle is a longer lever and takes
more time to move in the sweeping arc
than in the screw roll

7.14 The pawlata.

than with the screw roll. The hands are moved from their normal
paddling position. The pawlata is sometimes used as a progression to learning the screw roll but with either of these rolls, by
moving your hand position along the length of the paddle shaft,
you can increase or decrease the paddle's leverage capabilities,
making it shorter or longer.

The movements are exactly the same as for the screw roll but
the position of the hands on the paddle is different. The control

blade (right) is still flat or horizontal and is near the bow of the kayak, but the non-control blade is close to the hip. Hold the bottom corner of the non-control blade at your hip with your left hand. Your right hand holds the shaft a little way in front of the blade with the normal paddling grip on the shaft, just in a different place.

The paddle moves in the same arc as the screw roll when you are upside down, but it may just take a little longer to get the paddle into position because it is a longer lever to move around. Keep the paddle tight against the side of the boat as you capsize to help keep it in place. Get into the same set-up position as with the screw roll and then do the same movements to bring yourself back upright.

8

Rescues

Canoeing is a safe sport. There are very few fatalities in canoeing but there are correlations between accidents and inexperienced paddlers. Ignorance is not an excuse but a potential death trap. Safety is an attitude that you should have towards the water, based on the respect for what can happen if things go wrong.

As this is a book for beginners, white water rescues will not be covered. There are, however, important pieces of white water safety equipment and information that you at least need to know and have a basic understanding of, as your skill level will no doubt increase if you are keen and want to progress to more diffi-cult water. What will be covered in this chapter are rescues that will give beginners a good grounding from which to progress, with some information specifically related to white water.

The type of rescue, when needed, will be determined by the sit-uation, number and experience of people available and where you are. Assuming that you are paddling in a group of three or more, then there should be people to help. Rescue methods should always be practised and you should be confident of getting into and out of your canoe in all kinds of situations so that when it happens for real, it becomes an incident rather than an emergency. Make sure you are in safe water (such as a swimming pool) when you practice these rescues, so that you do not become an emer-gency yourself, or passers-by do not think you need help.

Rescue priorities

Good practice is to work on the assumption that you will rescue yourself. Never assume someone else will do it for you. Giving help to someone else, however, should be done in an order of

Reach

Throw

Tow / Row

Go yourself

8.1 This sequence of Reach, Throw, Tow/Row and Go yourself is the basic priority of any water rescue.

priority, something like this:

1. Reach.

2. Throw.

3. Tow.

4. Go yourself .

This does not mean that you physically go through this order, it means that there are different ways of tackling rescues, some methods being simpler or more appropriate than others, but this depends on the circumstances.

What to do after a capsize

If you capsize and come out of your canoe it is better to hang onto it, as it is buoyant, will give you support and help you to be seen by others. You should only abandon your canoe if there is a hazard that makes it more dangerous to stay with it and the potential for this happening is really only likely to be in white water. So take a breath and work out what you should do. If the water is cold it will drain your energy fast so you need to decide quickly.

If you are separated from your canoe

If you become separated from your canoe, but you have made it to the shore, then one of your party could push your canoe to the shore with the nose of their canoe. If you are in the water then you are more important than your canoe and should be helped by one of your party first. That could also mean being pushed, towed or helped to shore on the end of their canoe.

There are many different methods of towing, which on still, calm water are relatively simple to do. A rope is clipped onto the grab handle of the canoe that needs assistance, from the paddler doing the towing, then the tow commences. Having a quick release system on the body of the paddler doing the towing is important as they need to be able to escape from it if anything goes wrong. The paddler who is being towed can help by paddling as well.

Capsize and swimming

This next section on capsizing and what to do afterwards is not intended to put you off from paddling more gentle beginner's white water, but to inform you of what you need to be able to do to be safe in all grades of white water. The responses that you need to make have to become totally instinctive and second nature, which only happens with training and practice. Experienced paddlers who rarely fall out of their canoes, are often the least experienced at swimming in an unexpected capsize, as they rarely get the practice. So practice in safe white water first so when it happens for real you are trained to respond automatically.

After a capsize in white water – keep your feet up, lie on your back and keep your feet downstream.

After a capsize:

- Keep your feet and hips up and very close to the surface.

- Go to the UPSTREAM end of your boat so you are not caught between the boat and an obstruction. If you are in a rapid and cannot get upstream of the boat, push it away from you and leave it.

- Lie on your back, with your feet downstream of your body.

- Decide which bank to go for and SWIM AGGRESSIVELY towards it.

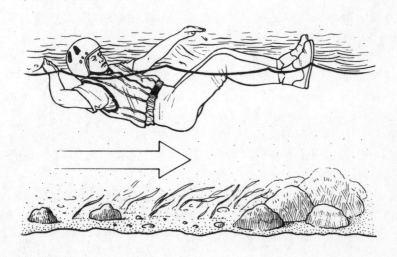

8.2 After a capsize in white water keep your feet up, lie on your back and keep your feet downstream. This is the safest way to swim in moving water.

I cannot stress the actions listed on page 119 enough. What you are avoiding is entrapment, which is getting your feet trapped in the river or you caught between your boat and an obstruction. With your feet up and downstream of your body, you can use them to fend yourself off rocks as you drift down.

Only stand up if your bottom is scraping on the ground. Do not stand up in white water when the water depth is above your knees. All people get knocked over very fast. If you are in water above your knees, or close to your knee height, and your feet get caught in the river, you can be knocked over instantaneously by the current and could possibly be held down with your head underwater.

The throw bag

The throw bag is a device that is designed to be an easy way of throwing a rope to someone, quickly and accurately, with a minimum of practice. The throw bag is one of the most useful items of river safety and rescue equipment. At some point you may need to throw one to help someone else get out of trouble or be thrown one yourself, so you need to know what they are and how to use one.

The throw bag is usually some form of lightweight but durable bag which contains the rope. A loop of the rope is secured to the outside of one end of the bag, and the rest of rope prevented from escaping out of the other by a quick release system. The rope contained in the throw bag should be a buoyant rope made of a soft material about 15–25m (50–80ft) long with a minimum diameter of 9mm (⅓in).

At the bottom of the bag there should be a fixed piece of buoyant closed-cell foam, which will keep the bag afloat once it has been thrown into the water.

How to use a throw bag

Throwing: The rope must be able to run freely from the bag, snaking its way out without coming out all at once. Release the securing system at the top, take some rope out and hold the end of the rope in one hand and the throw bag in the other. Throw the bag itself – underarm for short throwing distances and over-arm for longer distances (over about 15m or 50ft).

Aiming: Wait until the swimmer is at right-angles to you or just upstream of you, as this will be the shortest distance to throw. Shout loudly to the swimmer, before you throw the bag, to attract his or her attention. Throw the bag beyond them, but aim-ing to land the rope across their chest. It is better to aim slightly upstream of their body for two reasons; the rope will float faster and catch up with them and, when they reach for the rope, they can still keep their feet up. Reaching forwards lowers the feet and risks entrapment.

If you miss your target first time, pull the rope back in and either quickly recoil the rope or fill the bag with water and throw that. It will not travel as far but is worth a go.

After the rope is caught: As the thrower you need to be ready to do one of two things: take the strain that will come onto the rope and allow the swimmer to swing in towards the bank; or, if they look like they are being held under the current for too long because it is strong, move quickly but carefully down the bank while still holding the rope to swing them in lower down.

Receiving: The thrower should shout loudly to the swimmer to attract his or her attention. As a swimmer, watch for the rescuer if you can. When you catch the throw rope hold it on your chest over your shoulder with your arms bent. You might initially be submerged for a moment but hang on. Stay on your back looking downstream and allow yourself to be swung sideways, in towards the bank.

If you are holding a canoe as well, try and hold both the throw rope and canoe's grab line in the same hand so you do not get pulled apart, but do not let go of the throw rope to do this.

8.3 Two person 'rafted' tow.

Some white water information
Towing

Using any form of attachment in white water from canoe to canoe or paddler to canoe can be life threatening and needs to be treated with extreme caution.

Towing in white water should only be done by experienced paddlers in the calmer, longer stretches of water, below any rapids. As a beginner though you may be helped by someone else who is more experienced. They may use a two person 'raft', which is a short, quick and simple tow. The paddler having difficulties faces the rescuer, leans across the rescuer's canoe and holds on to both canoes, keeping them close together, while the rescuer paddles to a suitable place. The paddler who is being towed can help steer by pivoting their canoe slightly to one side or the other at the rescuer's request.

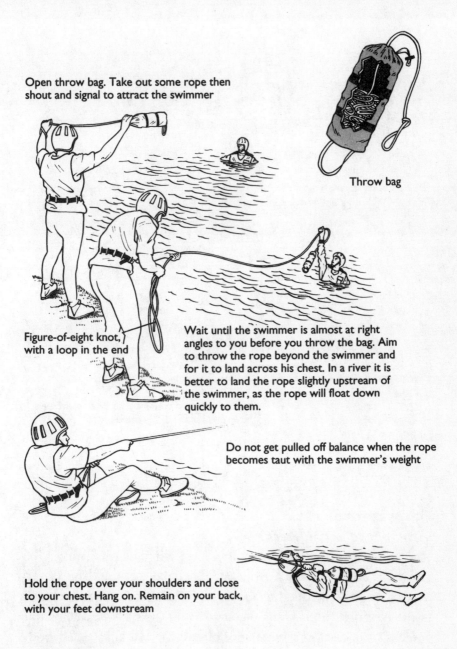

Open throw bag. Take out some rope then shout and signal to attract the swimmer

Throw bag

Figure-of-eight knot, with a loop in the end

Wait until the swimmer is almost at right angles to you before you throw the bag. Aim to throw the rope beyond the swimmer and for it to land across his chest. In a river it is better to land the rope slightly upstream of the swimmer, as the rope will float down quickly to them.

Do not get pulled off balance when the rope becomes taut with the swimmer's weight

Hold the rope over your shoulders and close to your chest. Hang on. Remain on your back, with your feet downstream

8.4 The throw bag.

The swimmer grabs the cockpit rim and paddler's wrist and clothing

Lean back to pull the kayak upright. Make sure the kayak is stable before you let go

8.5 Swimmer to kayak rescue.

Flat water rescues
Swimmer to kayak rescue
The swimmer to kayak rescue can be used when a paddler has capsized and for some reason stayed in their canoe. The swimmer, having reached the upside down kayak, leans over the centre of the upturned hull, grabs the cockpit on the far side, if possible grabbing the paddler's wrist or clothing as well and, using body weight, leans backwards pulling the kayak upright. Remember to stabilize the kayak before letting it go.

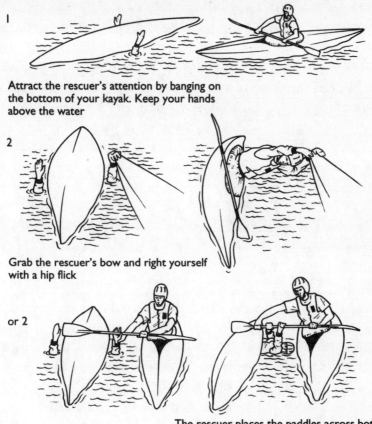

Attract the rescuer's attention by banging on the bottom of your kayak. Keep your hands above the water

Grab the rescuer's bow and right yourself with a hip flick

The rescuer places the paddles across both kayaks and then puts your hand onto the paddle for you to right yourself

8.6 Eskimo rescue.

Eskimo rescue

In reality this only happens if you are seen to go over by someone and both of you know what to do. However, to be rescued this way you need the confidence to hold your breath and keep yourself in your kayak by gripping tightly with your knees. Attract the attention of a rescuer by banging loudly on the bottom of your kayak. Keep your hands out of the water and be ready to grab hold of the bow of a canoe or a paddle.

The rescuer paddles towards your hands quickly, but in

control, so that neither you nor your canoe are damaged. You then grab the bow and right yourself with a hip flick, which is covered on pages 108-10. The rescuer needs to paddle gently towards your hands to prevent being pushed away. If the rescuer is using a paddle instead of the bow of their kayak, the rescuer moves alongside your kayak and places the paddle across both boats. Your nearest hand to the rescuer is placed, by him, onto the shaft of the paddle so that you can pull yourself upright. This method is safer than using the bow, as there is less chance of damage and the rescuer is also in a position to help you if you are hurt or tired. It is important that your hands are on the paddle between the canoes otherwise you will have difficulty in righting yourself.

X-rescue

This can be performed by one person in a kayak or open canoe alike and, if several people capsize, they can do this over each other's capsized canoes. This is an 'all in' capsize. If practised in safe water this type of capsize is good fun and good training.

The rescuer paddles to one end of the capsized canoe, reaches for this end while the canoe is upside down and carefully pulls it up and over the side of his canoe. Keeping the canoes at right-angles to each other will help make this easier. Then pull the canoe all the way across the deck using the decklines (or gunwales in open canoes) so that you can rock it empty. When it is empty place it back in the water beside you so the swimmer can climb back in.

Things to remember:

- As a rescuer, if you are in an open canoe and the other paddlers are cold, help them into your canoe before rescuing theirs.

- As a rescuer, if you are in a kayak, you should hold your paddle close to you because you will need it later on and do not want it to drift away.

- The swimmer should go to the bow of the rescuer's canoe so that they can easily be seen.

- As a rescuer, if you find doing the x-rescue difficult then the swimmer can help by going to the side of your canoe opposite to the capsized canoe and holding on to the side of the cockpit or gunwale. This provides some stability by counter-balancing the weight of the rescuer, who is leaning the other way.

There are many different ways to empty canoes which are swamped and awkward, as well as different ways to get back into them, which further reading and asking other, more experienced paddlers will reveal.

Getting back into the canoe and kayak

Place the kayaks so they face each other and depending on the ability of the swimmer they can enter in a variety of ways:

Getting back into the boat:

- The standard way is from between both kayaks getting the feet in first while leaning the body back in the water. The rescuer holds the paddles across both kayaks braced for stability, with hands holding each side of the cockpit.

- The swimmer gets into the canoe from the far side to the rescuer. In a kayak the paddles are put across both kayaks again and are used for stability. It is easy for the rescuer to help stabilize the nearest side of the kayak or open canoe for the swimmer when he or she enters at the middle of an open canoe and the cockpit of a kayak.

Rafted x-rescue

The x-rescue can also be done with two canoes rafted together for extra stability. This is more effective at times where a straightforward x-rescue may not be, such as in bad weather, but it does require co-ordinating another canoe to help. The principles are the same as for the x-rescue except that another canoe is rafted alongside the rescue boat to give additional support and help.

Open canoe

Kayak

Pull the boat across to empty it

Lift the boat up

Turn the boat over and slide it back into the water

Swimmer climbs back in

8.7 X-rescue.

Hi rescue

The hi rescue is used in similar circumstances to the rafted x-rescue and is probably more stable. It needs two rescuers. Each rescuer positions his or her kayak facing the same way, on either side of the capsized kayak. The paddles are used to make a bridge between the rescuers' kayaks. The two rescuers lift one end of the capsized kayak up and over the paddles, which are held firmly and close to the bodies of the rescuers. The kayak can now be

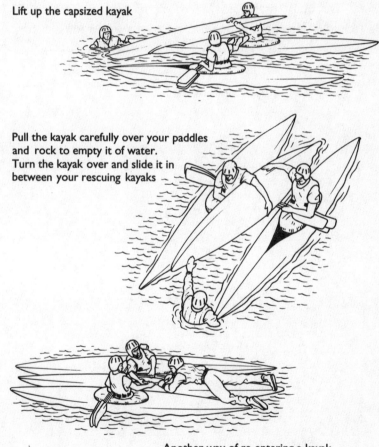

Lift up the capsized kayak

Pull the kayak carefully over your paddles
and rock to empty it of water.
Turn the kayak over and slide it in
between your rescuing kayaks

Another way of re-entering a kayak

8.8 Hi rescue (kayak).

rocked empty over the paddles then turned right way up and put back in the water for the swimmer to climb back in. An alternative way of getting back into the kayak is for the swimmer to get onto the back deck of his own canoe and edge his way along to the cockpit. The paddles are used for stability in the same way as in the other methods of entry.

If you have the presence of mind to lift the bow over the paddles first this will make emptying the kayak easier, as there should be less water to empty out of the stern because there is more buoyancy there than in the bow.

There are many variations of these rescues and the limit for ideas is really determined by your creativity and improvization.

9

Introduction to white water

Whatever your ultimate goal, before you begin paddling on white water there are various skills and information that you need to have, so you know how to handle white water safely. The current in white water, no matter how easy or innocuous it looks, is powerful and does not give in. When you stop paddling, the current will carry you along wherever it chooses. Good paddling skills avoid most problems, so sound basic canoe handling control is a necessary prerequisite for progressing on to white water.

Canoes, equipment and you

Chapter 2 will tell you what you need to do to make you and your equipment safe for use on white water. In this chapter river language and terminology, river features, basic moving water techniques and safety will be covered. Reading more advanced books on white water, going on white water canoeing courses run by BCU qualified canoeists, joining clubs and paddling with suitably experienced people will all add to your knowledge and experience. Do not be afraid of teaching yourself white water techniques, but do be very cautious and safe. Understand the medium which you are in, know your limitations and gain the knowledge and experience of appropriate safety and rescue techniques. Your education is your responsibility, but safety must come first.

Preparing yourself well is important on white water because as soon as you begin your descent you initiate a chain reaction of events. Decisions need to be made quickly and if a bad one is made problems can occur just as fast. It is not only big water that is dangerous. Even on what is known as easy water, canoes and people can be pinned against obstructions, such as walls and trees, by surprisingly small volumes of water. A current flowing at 3–4km an hour (2–3 miles per hour) can pin a canoe or person and hold the paddler underwater against an obstacle, overpowering a 6kg (13lbs) buoyancy aid.

Places to learn

Choose the right place, bearing in mind all the information in Chapter 3. The section of water you choose should not be huge or fast flowing or in flood conditions. Choose a site that you can check has no hazards such as weirs, trees or bushes in the water, either overhanging or otherwise. Watch out for metal stakes, fence posts and wires which could lie in, over or under the water. Steep or slippery banks should be avoided. Can you see the whole stretch of water that you want to use or are there bends?

Imagine what would happen if you capsized. Where could the river take you and how quickly? Would you have time to swim to a bank before the next hazard? Throw sticks onto the surface and see where they end up. Pick places where the flow is easy to see and is clearly defined, such as beside two strongly defined eddies at the bottom of some small rapids with a good stretch of calm water beneath them. The calm stretch is to allow you time to swim to the shore to rescue yourself if you should capsize, or to allow one of your party to help you get to the shore.

The eddies should be big enough for you to turn your canoe into and the river at least as wide as this. If the river is too narrow then the canoe will always be in different currents which will be confusing for you as a beginner.

Reading white water

In rapids the combinations of rocks, fast water and waves create particular patterns on the water which are reasonably predictable in all kinds of situations. Understanding what the patterns mean is what reading white water is all about.

Looking at the water and how it moves tells you what it is doing. The view that you get from a bank or place above the river is quite different from what you see at water level, sitting in your canoe. When you have viewed the overall features from above, squat down at canoe height to try and get a view of what you will probably see as you paddle. Give yourself as much chance as possible to recognize these features from your canoe. For example, you will not be able to see behind a rock that is 1m (3ft) high in the river, as the height of your eyes will be close to the height of the rock. With time and practice, reading the river from your canoe will improve, but there will always be

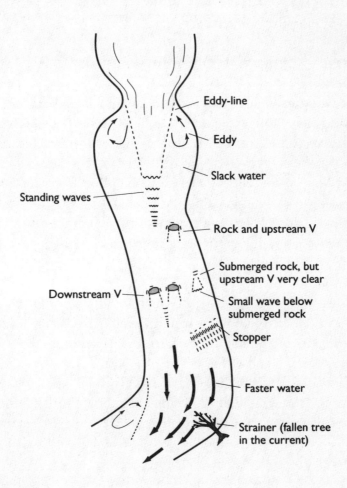

9.1 River features.

times when you need to get out of your canoe to see what is ahead. If you have any doubt or uncertainty whatsoever, it is good and safe practice to get out of your canoe and take a look.

River flow

The speed at which water flows in a river varies greatly not only during or after rainfall, but also across the width of a river. Even on a straight section the flow is faster in the middle than at the sides due to friction with the river banks. Likewise deeper channelled water is faster too, the surface being furthest away from friction with the river bed.

River language, terminology and hazards

Bends

Moving water likes to travel in straight lines until it hits something and changes direction, as it does on bends. The strongest current, therefore, flows towards the outside of bends and gets progressively weaker towards the inside. As a result there is more erosion on the outside of bends, exposing tree roots and undercutting rocks and creating the potential for more hazards. So, in general, treat bends with caution. Approach them slowly and on the inside until you can see a clear route through.

Rocks

Rocks are usually easier to find in white water because they create a particular wave pattern which locates their position. In slow-moving water the surface reveals nothing about the rocks underneath, but as the speed of water increases the rocks cause formation of a curling wave right behind and downstream of them. This wave will grow correspondingly in height and power as the amount of water flowing over the rock also increases.

Trees

Trees often grow in abundance on river banks, which means that they overhang into the current and fall across it, either completely or partially causing a nasty hazard. Especially when the river level is high, what was normally clear of overhanging branches and trunks may well put a canoeist up in the boughs. If you capsize and end up going for a swim stay well clear of trees. They are not known as 'strainers' for nothing!

Weirs

Weirs are artificial steps or ledges constructed in some rivers to help regulate and control the flow of water. The materials used to make the weirs include wood, stone, concrete and steel. Some weirs have artificial ledges at the bottom to prevent the erosion of the river bed.

Weirs are very common and some can be canoed safely but most are very dangerous. Given time, the materials used to construct the weir erode away leaving things such as stakes, edges and holes that can trap a canoe or swimmer. These hazards are not always visible.

The only way to be sure that a weir is free of such traps is to look at it with no water running over it. Check the bottom of the drop in particular, as this is where most erosion occurs. This does not mean that the weir is then safe because the shape of a weir also varies, the only common feature being that they cross the river. Some weirs are symmetrical and this is a perfect shape for creating dangerously powerful, re-circulating stoppers which can hold a canoe and swimmer. It is not at all easy to assess the movement of water at the bottom of a weir and to say confidently that a swimmer will be able to get out easily, if at all. Even if it is considered to be safe at one water level, it certainly does not mean that at other levels it can also be called safe. In higher water levels or flooding, many weirs considered to be otherwise safe are killers.

Even experienced canoeists have difficulty in assessing the dangers accurately. Just because someone else has gone through all right does not mean that the weir is safe to run. The only way to be sure is to stay well clear.

Bridges

The upstream side of a bridge pillar or support is a dangerous place to be because being caught sideways, across the front of the pillar, will result in the canoe being easily pinned or wrapped around it. Keep well clear.

Eddies

Because water likes to travel in straight lines, when it flows past obstacles such as a rock or part of the bank jutting out into the flow, it leaves a flat, calm spot immediately behind the obstacle, called an eddy. If the water flows strongly past the obstacle then the water in the eddy curls back on itself and flows upstream. It is a bit like blowing smoke away from your face – the main flow goes away from you but there is always some that curls back on itself, towards you. The border that is formed between the main current and the eddy is called the eddy-line.

Eddies are very useful places on a river and can be found in varying sizes behind any obstruction. Eddies are useful for getting in and out of your canoe, for taking a rest from the main current, or as places from which to check the next section of water to see what it holds in store.

Waves

Waves mean energy and are formed when there is a sudden increase in the flow of water in the current. There are two main types of waves: standing waves which occur in the strong down-stream Vs; and stoppers which are formed by water pouring over an obstruction.

Standing waves can have different tops to them – smooth hump-back ones are formed in places with less energy in the cur-rent; breaking crests form where the increase in flow is great enough to force the wave to grow beyond its maximum height so that the top collapses, falling down on its front.

Rapids can have a mixture of different types of standing waves. Several standing waves, one after the other, form a 'wave train';

they are good news and indicate where to go. Large standing waves are generally associated with fast, deep water so following them will usually keep you away from rocks.

Stoppers are formed when water pours abruptly over an obstruction such as a rock or weir. The fast-moving water pours over the obstruction, hits the water at the bottom and continues on down, below the surface, until its power decreases. In the act of doing this, the falling water creates a slot or hole in the water immediately below the obstruction that it falls into.

The laws of nature then dictate that the hole caused by the falling water must be filled immediately and this is done with more water in the form of a foaming wave crashing back in on itself, a bit like a vertical eddy. This foaming wave is known as a stopper, so called because the force of the wave crashing back upstream on itself can stop a canoe. Some stoppers are no problem at all but others can be fatal, especially ones that form at the bottom of some weirs.

There are many variations on the same basic shapes of waves which can have different effects on canoes. One of the hardest things to do is to be able to distinguish between them in white water when the formations join together, especially in the more difficult rapids.

Does a stopper smile or frown at you?

I like to view stoppers as if they are mouths on a face, as I will explain in a moment. First some more information to help you to understand how and why stoppers can be compared to mouths.

Water moves in a stopper not only up and down, but sideways and backwards and forwards as well. This sideways direction or movement of water in the foaming wave is also the easiest direction to move in (if you get caught) as you are going with the flow of water. This natural direction of flow is known as the stopper's kick. The kick may also be used to determine the consequences of a swim and help you to decide whether the stopper is worth attempting to canoe through or not.

The shape of the stopper as a mouth, is viewed as you are looking downstream. Some look happy and smile, others turn down at the corners, some are just tight-lipped and horizontal, others are straight and angled and some pull all kinds of contortions. Smiling stoppers are safest for canoeists and swimmers. If you get caught or held in a smiling stopper there is more chance of escaping at the sides, via the happy and up-turned corners, that is going with the kick – the natural flow of water.

The other stoppers go with the expression of human emotion as well. Frowning or downward turned corners will more than likely direct you to the centre of the stopper's mouth and hold you there (unless you are lucky enough to find a crack and it dribbles you out). Escape via the corners in the downward turned mouth is not always possible as getting to the corners is going against the kick.

The tight- or straight-lipped stopper with an angle variety, will direct you to the more happy corner, which if angled upwards and downstream will allow you to escape that way. But if it is straight and boxed in, like in a concrete-sided weir, then you have little chance of escape. Finally if you are caught in a contorted-mouth stopper, find the downstream creases in the mouth for your escape. Happy stoppering! Keep smiling downstream!

Downstream and upstream Vs
The words downstream and upstream refer to the direction in which the point of the V is aiming, a bit like an arrow head. For a downstream V, as you paddle down the river you approach the wide part first and the point of the V next. These indicate deeper water and clear paths or channels down the river. An upstream V is caused by an obstruction in the river. The point of the V is formed by an obstruction and points at the obstruction. To the side of the wide part of the V is where the eddy will be, as water flows past the obstruction in its straight line path. Avoid the point of the upstream V so you do not get caught on the obstruction which may be hidden under the surface. Two obstructions in the

water will each have an upstream V, but between them the edges of their Vs will form a downstream V and indicate the deeper channel to pass through.

Rapids

Rapids are sections of turbulent water in varying degrees of difficulty, made up of waves, rocks, eddies, downstream and upstream Vs. The water is turbulent because it is descending and being compressed by a narrowing in the channel that it is passing through, such as in a gorge or over shallow ground.

River grades

Rapids vary enormously in their difficulty and are graded in six general categories from I-VI. However, there are limitations to the grading system as it is a subjective one and leaves scope for disagreement. The grading does not take into account the width of the river or its volume of water. What some call a grade III others will call a grade IV and vice versa.

Inspecting rapids

Inspecting rapids is important for gaining information about potential hazards and to look for the safest or best way through them. As a beginner your rapids should be very straightforward and easy to negotiate, but as your skill level progresses you should know that there are many things you need to take into consideration before running any old rapid.

To inspect a rapid, study the water from the bank:

- What are the hazards to the canoe and to swimmers?
- Where is the route?
- Where do you need protection and what do you need?
- What will happen if the canoe capsizes?
- Where could the canoe be sent or get caught?

Look at the land around the river for clues to what you may find in the river bed. Look for rock ledges, geological changes, narrowing of the river and gorges. Expect drops or falls in these situations. What is the river bed composed of? Rounded boulders, sharp slate, rock ledges, pot holes. These all indicate the potential for canoes and people getting caught or hung up if swimming.

The best way to learn is with experienced white water paddlers who will be able to point things out to you and explain what they mean. And if you relate what you see to your past experience you will get a feeling for whether you want to run a rapid or not.

Moving water techniques

Having found a suitable place to learn the basic white water skills there are a few manoeuvres that you need to know in order to get into, out of and across the current. These are the break-in, break-out and ferry glide respectively. These manoeuvres use the eddies and current to turn the canoe, saving as much energy as possible by getting the moving water to do the work.

In an open canoe the canoe needs to be trimmed so that the bow rides slightly higher than the stern. To do this, either put more weight in the stern or move your positions slightly, changing places if necessary.

Getting into your canoe

Choose a very gentle part of the current, where the water is moving but with less turbulence, and get into your canoe facing upstream in an eddy or slack water, so that you do not drift off before you are ready. Keep your paddle across your canoe in front of you while you sort yourself out. When you paddle away from the bank and into the current, there are two things that the current will try to do: it will try and spin the canoe round and it will try and tip the canoe over. The first is controlled by breaking-in and breaking-out and the second is controlled by edging and leaning on the downstream side.

You will find that when you leave the eddy or slack water and cross into the current, the current will spin the canoe and the canoe may tip, which at first feels a little unstable. This is now the time to practise edging and leaning which were covered in Chapter 7. The technique of edging the canoe and leaning the body downstream is important in white water to prevent you capsizing upstream. Edging is used each time that the canoe is angled across the current and leaning is used in the same situations, but the amount of lean will depend on the speed of the turn and how tight it is.

Crossing the current – ferry glide

This method (used by many river ferries) is the simplest way of crossing the current and can be done either facing upstream and paddling forwards, which is easier, or facing downstream and paddling backwards which is more strenuous. The aim of the ferry glide is not to lose any ground downstream.

In a ferry glide two things will affect your speed and direction across the current: how fast you paddle and the angle of your canoe to the current. The more you point your canoe across the current the faster you will turn downstream. It is the angle in relation to the canoe and the current that is important, not the angle between the canoe and the bank. Working out how best to get across the current is therefore a combination of the right speed and angle.

Forward ferry glide (kayak and open canoe)

- Face the canoe upstream along the bank.

- Move out of the slack water by paddling forwards or sideways with the canoe angled slightly into the main current.

- Once in the current, set your canoe's angle and speed by trial and error, paddling forwards in a kayak and combining forward strokes, draws and prys in an open canoe. If you find that the canoe turns too far downstream, use sweep strokes in a kayak to bring it back to the right angle and a combination of sweeps, draws and prys in an open canoe. If in doubt about what angle to set, then start off with a narrow angle, as it is easier to open up and make wider than it is to reduce it and recover.

- Remember to edge the canoe slightly when it is angled across the current.

- Practise crossing the river from both sides.

Reverse ferry glide (kayak and open canoe)

The same techniques apply for the reverse ferry glide as for the forward ferry glide. The reverse ferry glide is important for the beginner to practice well, as it is this manoeuvre that is often used: to avoid obstacles which suddenly appear directly downstream in front of the canoe; and to slow down and give the paddler more time to work out what is ahead.

So to practise the reverse ferry glide:

- Move into the current, either sideways or backwards.

- Look over your downstream shoulder.

- Set a narrow angle and use wide backward strokes for control as they are more stable.

- Edge the canoe slightly downstream.

- In an open canoe the bow paddler maintains the angle by steering, using a combination of sweep stokes, draws and prys.

- Practise the manoeuvre, crossing the river from both sides.

To use the reverse ferry glide to avoid obstacles which suddenly appear downstream and directly in front of you, point your bow at the impending obstruction and paddle backwards away from it. Pointing your bow at the obstruction ensures that you will not get caught across it sideways.

Instinct will probably tell you to paddle like crazy keeping the same direction, but just paddling faster means that there is still a chance you could get caught.

Forward ferry glide

The angle of the ferry glide

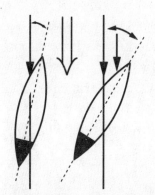 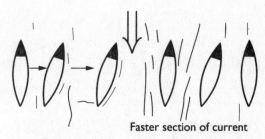

Faster section of current

Draw away from the bank, setting your angle by paddling forwards. Adjust the angle as the speed of the current changes

Narrow angle   Wide angle to
to the current   the current

A wider angle means more water pushes against your 'exposed' bow so you have to paddle faster to get across the current. If the current is fast, use a narrow angle to control your speed

Reverse ferry glide to avoid obstructions

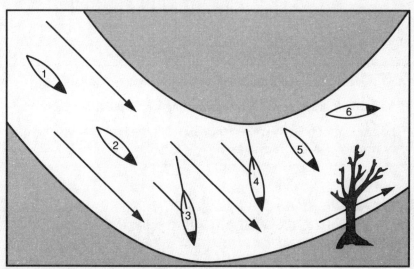

The canoe appears to be sideways on to the obstruction, but it is the angle of the canoe relative to the current that is important

9.2 Forward and reverse ferry glide.

Eddy-line spirals

This is an exercise which uses the two opposing currents that make up the eddy-line to deliberately spiral the canoe down the eddy-line and feel the effect that the different currents have. Select an eddy-line that is not too powerful, but is well defined, and gently paddle the canoe so that it is about halfway across both currents. Start as high up the eddy-line as you can to give yourself the maximum distance you could travel. You may need to do some strokes to keep the canoe from slipping off the eddy-line, but try and feel what happens to each end of the canoe as it passes through the currents. Keep the canoe's momentum by assisting the turns with gentle sweep strokes to spiral the canoe down as far as you can.

Breaking-in and breaking-out

Collectively the turning into and out of the current is called an eddy-turn and good eddy-turns have several components to them, three of which, if you get them right, mean you hardly need to use your paddle to complete the turn.

Good eddy-turns depend on:

- The angle that you approach and enter the eddy or current.

- The momentum that you have for getting into the eddy or current.

- The amount of edge that the canoe has and the lean that you have when you cross the eddy-line.

The break-in

The principles are the same for both the kayak and open canoe, but the tandem open canoe has to use different strokes from the kayak owing to the style of paddling and because there is the option of paddling on different sides. The kayak being a shorter canoe will turn more easily than the open canoe and to turn the canoe well requires efficient use of the current.

The break-in is used when you want to move from the eddy into the current and then paddle downstream. What you need to do first, and what is often quite difficult for a beginner, is to decide exactly where the eddy-line is, as it is the border between the eddy and the current. Sometimes this is very distinctive and at other times less so. However the border will be at its most obvious close to the obstruction that the current is flowing past. Once you have found the border, you can make a break-in.

Make a break into the current by:

- Picking up speed across the eddy, aiming to hit the eddy-line at an angle of about 45 degrees.

- Making sure that you have enough momentum to cross the eddy line.

- As the nose of the canoe crosses the eddy-line, edge the canoe by lifting the upstream side and lean your body, if it is necessary, downstream.

Kayak

In a kayak the emphasis for breaking-in needs to be on using edge control of the canoe and body lean, depending on the strength of the current. Initiate the turn with a sweep stroke. As you cross the eddy-line, edge the kayak, leaning if necessary, and be ready to use a low-brace turn if needed. The kayak will turn downstream. As you finish the turn, bring the kayak back to a level position and continue paddling forwards, downstream.

Open canoe

In a tandem open canoe, do a low-brace turn on the downstream side when the paddle on the downstream side crosses the eddy-line. Trust your partner to help with the edging and lean. The bow paddler, if not doing the low-brace turn, can do two things: a sweep stroke to initiate the low-brace turn as soon as the bow crosses the eddy-line and help with edging and leaning; or a cross-bow cut to help the turn and help with the edging.

If the bow person is doing the low-brace turn, the stern person initiates the low-brace turn with a sweep stroke and then helps with the edging and leaning. As the turn is finished, bring the canoe back to its level position and continue paddling forwards. If paddling solo, either use a low-brace turn or a cross-bow cut, on your respective side, as your body crosses the eddy-line. Both of these strokes are initiated with a sweep stroke.

In open canoes there is nothing wrong with paddlers deciding on which side they would like to paddle to make the best use of their strokes, before the canoe is moved into the current. After all we do have our preferred sides.

More hints on breaking-in
Whether you are paddling an open canoe or a kayak, make sure that when you break-in to the current and use your paddle to support you, that both your body and paddle are over the current that you are turning into, otherwise the turn becomes less efficient and less stable. This is where your edge, lean and

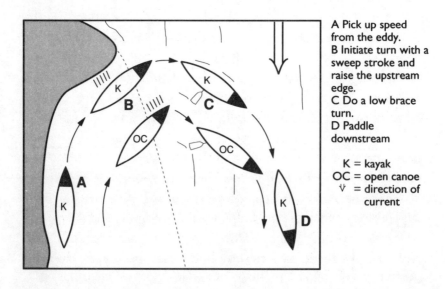

A Pick up speed from the eddy.
B Initiate turn with a sweep stroke and raise the upstream edge.
C Do a low brace turn.
D Paddle downstream

K = kayak
OC = open canoe
⇕ = direction of current

9.3 The break-in.

momentum play their part in making efficient use of the currents to turn the canoe.

The momentum that you need to cross the eddy-line depends on the speed of the current. Generally the faster the current the more momentum required to break through the eddy-line.

If the angle of the canoe is too narrow when you leave the eddy, you will probably cross the eddy-line into the current and end up pointing upstream but not turning. If the angle is too wide you probably will not completely cross the eddy-line but will stay on the edge of it and maybe spiral downstream a little.

Break-in without using your paddles

Angle and momentum are somewhat allied. If you leave or enter an eddy with a narrow angle and close to the obstruction, then generally you will require less momentum to cross the eddy-line than if you enter or leave the eddy with a wide angle and lower down. Practise in a slow moving current without using your paddles. Use your paddles to set up a good angle, momentum and edge, but then hold your position and balance and take your paddles out of the water. You will find that if you get everything right, the canoe will turn of its own accord. Not using your paddles to make the turn will improve your technique as it means that you are using the current to do the work for you.

Problems that you may encounter when not using your paddles:

- If your momentum slows before you have turned into the current sufficiently, then on the next attempt increase your angle. If you turn before you are completely across the current, reduce your angle.

- If you overshoot into the current but eventually turn, then you have too much momentum, so slow down. If you do not make it to the current then go faster.

- Just edge the canoe, do not lean your body, as you will not have your paddle to support you. If you do not edge the canoe enough it will be unstable, if you edge too much, have your paddle ready to support you!

The break-out

The break-out is moving from the current into an eddy. You may want to do this for several reasons – to take a break, to get out and check a rapid, to let others catch up with you and so on. The break-out has exactly the same principles as the break-in and in the same order: angle, momentum, edge and lean. Once you have decided on the eddy that you want to use, then get your canoe aggressively into position as soon as possible.

The most important thing in breaking-out is giving yourself enough time to spot the eddy you want to use, so you can set yourself up in the right position. If you do not give yourself adequate time, you will miss the eddy faster than you would think possible. Early anticipation is the key to the break-out so that you have enough time to get the canoe onto the right float-lines.

Float-lines

Float-lines are lots of imaginary lines on the water going with the current. Imagine you are a stick floating in the current on the surface, being positioned on the right float-line means that the lines of current that you are on will drift you naturally to where you want to be. So if your canoe is facing across the current then it will be across lots of float-lines. If it is pointing upstream or downstream it will be covering less float-lines. The trick to making the break-out is for the canoe to be on the right float-lines as early as possible.

To prepare for the break-out aim as high up the eddy as you can. This means aiming just below the obstruction that is causing the eddy, but only enough so that you do not hit it. Your aim is to sneak in immediately behind the obstruction. Your canoe is now at the right angle.

Having got the right angle, paddle forwards towards your target. All you have to do is to gauge the right amount of momentum to end up at the top of the eddy. At this stage paddling aggressively is best. You can always slow down but you cannot always make up lost ground. The combination of the right

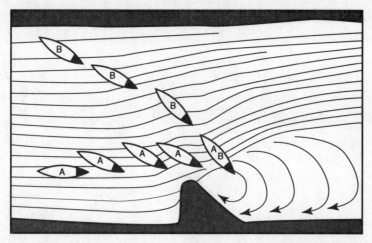

Canoe AB is where you want to end up. Canoe A is on the float-lines closest to the eddy early and as a result can almost float down into the eddy, using less momentum than canoe B. Canoe B needs to use more speed to cross several float-lines before getting into the best position close to the eddy in order to break-out. Both canoes, however, have a good angle. Note that when the canoe is facing across the current how the number of float-lines that it is on increases

9.4 Float-lines and different approaches to breaking-out.

angle and speed, and being on the right float-line should allow you easily to make it into the eddy.

Fine tuning of both the break-in and break-out comes with practice in getting the right timing and co-ordination of all aspects in each manoeuvre.

Break-out strokes (kayak)

Having arrived at the top of the eddy, initiate the turn with a sweep stroke on the downstream side of the kayak as soon as the bow crosses the eddy-line. Then immediately edge the kayak and lean into the turn with a low-brace turn. The kayak will spin quickly and, as the turn finishes, bring the kayak back level again.

Break-out strokes (open canoe)

The strokes will differ as much as in the break-in, but the moves are very similar. Having arrived at the top of the eddy, the stern

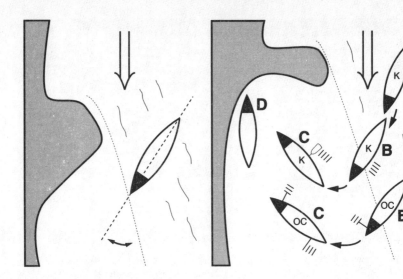

Being at the right angle is important when entering an eddy, especially in more difficult sized and shaped eddies

Key

K = kayak

OC = open canoe

↓ = direction of current

↶ = low-brace turn

⁄≋ = sweep stroke

↝ = bow cut or bow draw

A Get into the right angle and pick up the right amount of momentum

B and C Kayak – initiate turn with forward sweep. Edge the kayak and do a lowbrace turn into the eddy

B and C Open canoe – initiate the turn with a sweep stroke in the stern. Edge the canoe and do a bow cut or a bow draw.

D Be ready to paddle forwards to stay in the eddy

9.5 The break-out.

soon as the bow crosses the eddy-line. Do not forget to edge the canoe and lean into the turn as the bow paddler puts their paddle into the eddy to do a bow cut or a cross-bow cut. The bow will then be held in the eddy as the stern swings in. As the turn is completed, bring the canoe back to its level position and be ready to paddle forwards in case you slide back out of the eddy.

Eddy-setting

Eddy-setting is really like doing a reverse ferry glide into an eddy. It is used when the river is too narrow for a canoe to turn around to get into an eddy, or when there is not enough room between to get into an eddy, or when there is not enough room between the obstructions to turn the canoe through its length. Small spaces make it difficult or impossible to do a break-in, particularly with tandem open canoes as they are long and not very manoeuvrable. Eddy-setting is not however very effective in catching difficult eddies in deep, fast currents.

Prepare for an eddy-set when you see an eddy that you want to get into, again giving yourself plenty of time to get into position. Point the stern in the direction that you want to go and keep facing slightly downstream, but angled across the river. The angle will be the same as in a reverse ferry glide, because this is actually what you do. Again aim to be high up in the eddy, high enough so that the stern could just brush past the obstruction.

As soon as you have a good angle, paddle backwards to get onto the float-line that will take you to the eddy. Again aggressive paddling is better at first to get into position with the right momentum. The aim is to drop into the top of the eddy and, as soon as the stern brushes past the obstruction, quickly paddle backwards into the eddy and immediately edge the canoe in the same way you would if you were going forwards, presenting the hull to the eddy. Lean into the turn if necessary. This time the bow paddler initiates the turn with a reverse sweep stroke, a draw stroke, a cross-bow draw or a pry, while the stern paddler puts his or her paddle into the eddy using combinations of draw strokes, reverse sweeps or prys on his side. Again be ready to paddle backwards to stay in the eddy.

10

Other forms of canoeing

There are several different forms of canoeing which are generally classified into: touring, recreation and competition. Competition canoeing is further divided into eight different disciplines, and you do not have to be a potential world class paddler to take part as they are all graded to suit differing levels of ability. To tackle the competitions, however, you need to be insured which is covered either by paying a fee on the day or by being a member of the BCU.

The eight competitive disciplines are: sprint racing, slalom, marathon, wild water racing, canoe polo, rodeo and play-boating, and International 10 square metre canoe and there are a number of different types of kayaks and canoes that take part.

Sprint racing

This is one of the two Olympic canoeing events. It is done on flat water and takes place at regattas. The distances covered in the races are between 200m (220yd) and 1000m (1095yd) and include corners or turns which may be required in the longer distances. The racing is done in singles, doubles and fours in both open canoes (C1, C2, C4) and kayaks (K1, K2, K4). The sprint canoe has virtually no deck and is paddled by kneeling on one knee. In the sprint kayak the paddlers keep their knees together and wear spray-decks for warmth and protection.

The boats are long and narrow in order to go as fast as possible, but the maximum length, width and weight for each type of boat is controlled by regulations. Each boat has a foot-controlled rudder as a steering mechanism so that the paddler's synchronized rhythm remains smooth, with as little interruption as possible.

The main centre for racing in the UK is at Holme Pierrepont in Nottingham and the best way to get into sprint racing is through a club.

Slalom

Canoe slalom is probably the most well known aspect of canoe competition. It is an event run on a white water course over a distance of about 600m (660yd). The competitors have to pass through a series of 25 gates of two poles each, about 1.5m (5ft) apart hanging over the river. There is a set order and direction for each of the gates to be passed through and the object of the event is to do the course as fast as possible without incurring any time penalties. The penalties are added onto the time that a paddler takes to complete the course to produce an overall time. Each paddler has two timed runs on the course. The time penalties are 5 seconds added for touching the poles and 50 seconds for missing a gate or going through a gate the wrong way. The gates with red and white striped poles need to be passed through in an upstream direction and the green and white poles in a downstream direction. Some gates are passed through paddling forwards and others are passed through paddling backwards. Slalom canoes are also low volume so paddlers can dip the ends of them under the poles. The boats that take part are single-seater kayaks (K1) and single- or double-seater canoes (C1, C2). These canoes and kayaks are very manoeuvrable as they have a short water line length, however, slalom competition regulations control their minimum length and width. Strict safety regulations are enforced on both equipment and organization, with rescuers positioned in the appropriate places on the course. The UK is known as one of the leading slalom nations and usually does very well at World Championship slalom events.

Marathon

Marathon racing is similar to sprint racing but can be held on any type of natural waterway, either inland or on the sea, and often involves portaging the boat across obstructions such as dams or locks and crossing large lakes. The marathon event is open to any type of canoe or kayak within the size and weight dimensions specified in the International Canoe Federation regulations.

Most marathons begin with a mass start and the overall distances begin at about 6.4km (4 miles) for the lower divisions. The longest distance in the UK is 201km (125 miles) with 72 portages and is from Devizes to Westminster, London. The nine separate marathon divisions enable races to be run for every level of ability and, as the event can be run on any type of water in a wide range of boats, it is a popular sporting discipline.

Paddlers undertaking marathon competitions not only have to contend with the required level of paddling, but also have to co-ordinate their portages and other racing tactics such as hanging on the wash of other boats to save energy (but not power boats). Many paddlers fix pumps to their boats that are foot operated to keep the boat dry and no kind of assistance is allowed to be received by those taking part, except for the administration of food and drink. The exceptions to this are for disabled people who need help with portage.

Wild water racing

This particular branch of the sport requires a combination of the paddling skills used in many of the other disciplines. Wild water racing events are held on rivers over a distance of at least 3km (nearly 2 miles). They last about 30 minutes with rapids of up to grade IV or V. The boats that compete are K1, C1 and C2 and are similar in design to the sprint racers but need more volume and strength to cope with the powerful white water. Paddlers set off at about one minute intervals, choosing their own route down the river while competing against the clock. Paddling this event requires the combined skills of the marathon for endurance, the precision of the slalomist and the power of the sprinter. The art of paddling on fast water in this way and negotiating all the obstructions is a great skill and takes a long time to perfect.

Canoe polo

This is another canoeing event at which Britain excels and is a five-a-side team game played in very small kayaks called BATs (Baths Advanced Trainer). Helmets and full-length buoyancy aids are compulsory for protection as canoe polo is a close contact game. For safety reasons also the boats have very rounded ends and the tips of paddle blades must not have metal surrounds and need to be of a minimum thickness. Full face visors too, are sensible protection. Paddlers pass the ball between them, trying to avoid the opposition and score in their opponent's goal, which is a 1m (3ft 3in) square board or net suspended 2m (6ft 6in) above the water. The game can be played in any area of water allowing the regulation size pitch and goals. The ball may be stopped by the paddle but not projected by it and when a person is in possession of the ball the opposition are allowed to push paddlers off balance which often leads to a capsize.

Surf

Canoe surfing is a bit like gymnastics in a boat and is one of the two competitive canoe disciplines that does not compete against the clock. Paddlers get 20 minutes to impress the judges in their performance of various tricks and manoeuvres. As many moves as possible are linked together on one wave. The three highest wave scores give an overall total and the two paddlers with the highest scores for their heat go through to the next round. The judging is of course subjective, but paddlers' skills are evaluated against a set of criteria. Safety regulations are strict and include only one paddler on a wave at a time.

Rodeo and play-boating

This is similar to surfing in that there is no race against the clock and paddlers play on waves and stoppers on the sea or on rivers, trying to impress the judges. Usually events are held over one or two days with heats for six to eight paddlers. In periods of about 10–15 minutes the paddlers demonstrate their skill and ability in linking many exotically named moves and tricks together on the competition wave or stopper. The judges mark the performances and the two highest scoring paddlers go forward to the next round. Another way of being judged is 'head to head'. This is a process of eliminating the paddlers on their performance, until only two competitors are left to compete the final.

Unlike many of the canoe disciplines, however, in rodeo there are no divisions where you can start as a novice and progress upwards. Novices to rodeo compete alongside experienced competitors on the same water conditions, but are assessed in their novice class. This does seem to require a relatively high starting point for novice skill levels, or at least an ability to roll. There are two categories of boats that take part: the float boat and the squirt boat in both canoe and kayak. The float boat is the more popular, but any white water boat will suffice as rodeo events are aimed at everyday white water paddlers.

International 10 square meter canoe

Canoe sailing is one of the oldest forms of the sport from the days of John MacGregor who used a sail on his kayak in the 1860s. The International 10 square metre canoe is a very fast, single-handed sailing dinghy, highly developed for racing on the sea or inland open waters and is sailed competitively throughout the world. The shape of the 5.2m (17ft) long hull is strictly controlled by the class regulations and is powered by 10 square metres of sail (107.6 square feet). The helmsman has a sliding seat which is used to lean out on, to counteract the effect of the wind on the sail which heels the boat. The Sailing Challenge Cup, which was presented by the Royal Canoe Club in 1874, has been competed for annually (except for the war years) which makes it one of the oldest of trophies still competed for today.

BCU lifeguards

This aspect of canoeing is particularly concerned with canoe safety and rescue, and trains people to a state of proficient canoe handling to enable the paddler to help anyone having difficulty in the water. There are canoe lifeguard units which operate all round the UK and they have annual conventions and competitions for other units and for people who are interested in lifesaving using canoes. The lifeguards offer advice on safety and rescue concerned with kayaks and canoes and pursue the development of skills on safety awareness in canoeists.

Touring and recreation

Recreational canoeing is a sport that can appeal to paddlers of any age, ability and fitness. It includes all the competitive disciplines done non-competitively and can range from attempting adventurous, steep and mountainous rivers, or canoeing on gentle, sedate and non-moving lakes to working on surfing and rodeo moves for a challenge or paddling along the coast. Recreational canoeing is something that the whole family can enjoy and continue with into retirement.

There are many and various recreational and touring events organized throughout the year. These could be one- or two-day events or may involve an overnight camp. While these trips are led by experienced canoeists and all grades of paddlers are welcome, participants are expected to understand the implications of the conditions likely to be encountered on the grades of water for each trip undertaken.

Sea kayaking

Sea kayaking is one of the earliest forms of paddling. Archaeological evidence suggests that as far back as 5000 BC skilled hunters and fishermen were using 'highly developed craft' for their hunting and fishing vessels. Today, sea kayaking expeditions have been undertaken in some of the most dangerous seas in the world. The preparation, planning and timing of such trips, however, are all critical and integral to a trip's success or failure. Even then the unpredictable nature of the weather will often determine the outcome.

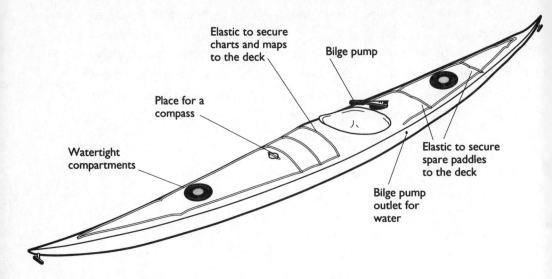

Elastic to secure
charts and maps
to the deck

Bilge pump

Place for a
compass

Watertight
compartments

Elastic to secure
spare paddles
to the deck

Bilge pump
outlet for
water

10.1 A sea kayak equipped with expedition hatches and fittings.

Sea kayaks

These are the more specialized kayaks for travelling on the sea. They are about 4.5-5.5m (14½–18½ft) long with double sea kayaks being a little bit longer. There are a variety of 'day boats' for people interested in short trips which are both stable when empty and roomy enough to carry equipment for a couple of days or so. Sea kayaks then increase in their size and volume with greater carrying capacities for longer trips or expeditions. Some larger kayaks are easier to handle than others and some are more suitable for rough conditions. Each sea kayak, like any other specialized boat, has its own handling characteristics and needs to be paddled in a variety of sea and weather conditions before deciding which one is the most suitable for which paddler.

Before going onto the sea, there are various factors that need to be considered. Not only do your paddling and rescue skills need to be proficient, but you also need to know a lot about tides, navigation and the weather, to name but a few. Conditions can change incredibly fast on the sea with the possibility of leaving you vulnerable and in a potentially dangerous situation.

As sea kayaking is such a huge topic and a sport on its own, more detailed information about aspects of it will be covered here. Such things as additional equipment needed, tides, navigation, rules of the road and weather will illustrate the depth of knowledge and information that is required when paddling on the sea.

Additional equipment for sea paddling

In sea kayaking, equipment is carried in addition to the equipment that you would carry in other aspects of the sport (this equipment is outlined in Chapters 4 and 10). Carrying distress flares, knowing how to use them and being aware of their limitations are important in case of an emergency. Red distress flares should be used in an emergency to attract attention to yourselves and your predicament, and to provide a homing signal for the rescue party. Even if the flares are used, however, there is no guarantee that you will be rescued as their function is dependent on them being seen by someone who also knows what to do. The sighting of the flare needs to be reported to the coastguard or police, before any form of action can be taken. Flares need to be carried somewhere where they can be easily found in an emergency, such as in the pocket of a buoyancy aid or in a bum bag. Red flares are for distress and white flares are for the prevention of a collision.

Other items of safety equipment that are carried on the sea are sometimes carried by canoeists on long journeys or open crossings. Two of these items are VHF radio telephones and Emergency Position Indicating Radio Beacons (EPIRBs), both of which are expensive and need careful looking after. Operating the radio also requires a VHF certificate of competence and a radio licence from the Home Office, and the beacons need constant checking to make sure that they are not accidentally switched on. The main drawbacks for canoeists using VHF radios are the batteries, which will inevitably need charging, and the radio's limited range and 'line of sight' transmission, as the canoe is so low on the water. When I have used a radio from a canoe to contact port or harbour authorities and so on, the communication has been successful, but trying to convince the authorities that we were just kayaks (or 'canoes') was a lot more difficult.

The authorities were not used to dealing with people sea kayaking using radios and so thought that our use of the word 'canoe' or 'kayak' was either to give the name of a motor-driven vessel, or the name of a canoeists' escort boat. The fact that there was no motor-powered vessel at all, just seemed to confuse them, so if you use radios be aware of the factors which limit their use for sea kayaking.

Tides

The tide is the rise and fall of the mass of water in the sea. This rise and fall is controlled by phases of the moon and the position of the moon in relation to the sun and earth. The movement of the sea varies enormously in strength and direction as it speeds up around headlands and through constricted areas (like on bends and in the shallows on a river). In both these cases waves and eddies are formed.

Where the sea crosses shallow ground these are called overfalls and where it races past a headland it is called a tidal race. These tidal forces can either work for the canoeist or against the canoeist, like the current in a river.

Not all places are affected by strong tidal streams, but knowing what speed the tide will reach is important. If there is a tidal stream rate (speed) of 3 knots (3 nautical miles an hour) and you are paddling with it you will travel at about 6 knots, but if you are against it you will paddle forwards through the water but not get anywhere. If the tidal stream rate was any faster you would actually travel backwards.

There are many names given to tides and their cycles, but as a sea paddler there are at least two that you need to understand the importance of. These are spring tides (or springs) and neap tides (or neaps). They are important because during these phases the tidal height (range) and speed (rate) varies considerably.

Spring tides occur at or near the time when there is a new moon and again when there is a full moon, which both happen when the sun, moon and earth are all in a straight line together. Neap tides occur at or near the time when the moon is about a half moon, which is when the sun and moon are at right-angles to the earth. What happens to the sea during spring tides is that the tidal stream rates will be stronger and faster than at neap tides and the heights of low and high water will be lower and higher making a greater tidal range. The word 'spring' has nothing to do with the season.

Obviously these different ranges and rates do not just suddenly happen. They are a cycle which slowly builds up and dies down, just as the moon gradually gets bigger (waxes) then smaller

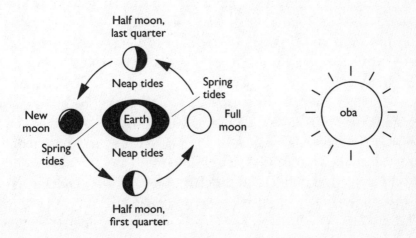

10.2 Spring tides occur when the moon, sun and earth are in a straight line with each other, when the gravitational pull is at its greatest.

(wanes). The phases of the moon and the tide happen at the same time – they are synchronous.

The tide generally flows for six hours in one direction, rising in height, which is called the flood tide and then reverses for six hours in the other, falling in height and is called the ebb tide. There are places that differ quite a bit from this generalization with some that have two 'high waters'. The tide also varies in time each day, as the moon's cycle round the earth takes almost 25 hours. This means that the tide is about 50 minutes later each day, so it is important to get the necessary information for each area and each day.

The twelfths rule (or 1,2,3–3,2,1 rule)

Another rule which is useful for sea paddlers, but often overlooked, is the twelfths rule or 1,2,3–3,2,1 rule. This is a method of estimating the approximate height of the tide during the six hours between high water and low water when it falls, or the six hours between low water and high water when it rises. This tidal range is divided into twelve parts: during the first and sixth hours water level rises (or falls) one-twelfth of the range; during the second and fifth hours the water level rises (or falls) two-twelfths; and during the third and fourth hours, the water level rises (or falls) three-twelfths. Not only does this tell us how deep the water may be for crossing over or landing on sand banks, but it also tells us the relative volume of water that will be moving at those particular hours. The third and fourth hours are when the most water is moving which means that during these two hours the tidal rate (speed) will be at its fastest and strongest. The twelfths rule is useful for sea paddlers as it is accurate enough and easy to remember and calculate. For example:

High water is 5.5m (18ft) and the following low water is 0.7m (2ft 3in)

In 2 hours 20 minutes after high water how much tide will have fallen?

Tidal range = 5.5 − 0.7m = 4.8m (15ft 9in)

In the first hour the tide falls $\frac{1}{12}$ of 4.8 = 0.4m (1ft 4in)

In the second hour tide falls $\frac{2}{12}$ of 4.8 = 0.8m (2ft 8in)

In 20 mins of the third hour tide falls $\frac{1}{3}$ of $\frac{3}{12}$ of 4.8 = 0.4m (1ft 4in)

Total fall = 1.6m (5ft 3in)

Basic navigation for sea kayaking

Navigation is the art and science of guiding a boat safely from one place to another using all the skills and instruments necessary. There are different types of navigation, the most simple being coastal navigation or pilotage which is when you are close to land and using visible objects as your guide. When you are out of sight of land or doing an open sea crossing you need to calculate in advance a good course to steer, bearing in mind the speed at which you travel and the rate and direction of the tides.

The main objective in navigation for sea paddlers is to take advantage of the tide as much as possible and, in order to plan that in advance, the information you will need can be found by using some or all of the equipment listed below.

Navigation aids

- Charts of the area; these are maps of the sea and sea bed. They contain lots of information on the sea including tidal races, overfalls, buoyage and tidal streams, but generally there is not much information about the land so they are good when used in conjunction with 1:50,000 maps of the area.

- 1:50,000 maps are good for working out camp-sites, towns for supplies, telephones, post offices, railways, roads and so on.

- Tide tables for your area are necessary for calculating high and low waters and the height of tides.

- A tidal stream atlas for your area will show in more detail the rate and direction in which the tide flows for every hour.

- Dividers or some means of accurately measuring distances on charts and maps.

- A compass, protractor or parallel rule for taking bearings off charts and maps.

- Coastal pilots are designed more for larger vessels and give details on tides and other relevant material such as facilities available in the area.

- Nautical almanacs. These are very comprehensive.

- Pencil, paper and rubber with which to make notes and calculations.

- A chinograph pencil or equivalent is useful to write important information on the deck of your kayak instead of on paper.

Coastal navigation or pilotage

This is like reading a road map in a car or navigating on the hills in clear weather. The maps and charts are read in the same way, using objects on the land or buoys in a shipping area to tell you where you are as you approach and go past them.

Transits

When paddling on the sea it is easy to believe that the direction in which you are facing and paddling is the direction in which you are moving. This may not be the case, however, and using transits in clear weather will reveal in which direction you are really going.

How to use transits

Use two prominent objects in line with you, one behind the other. These could be two headlands jutting out, a house and a buoy, a radio mast and some rocks and so on. If these are in front of you they will tell you your sideways movement. Watch them and try and keep them in position relative to each other. If the object at the back moves to the right, then to the right is the direction in which you are travelling and vice versa. To work out if the direction is forwards or backwards, watch two objects in line at your side in the same way and whichever direction the one behind moves, that is also your direction of travel.

Dead reckoning (DR)

This is a simple way of working out your approximate position without calculating the effect of the tide, if you know the course that you have steered and the distance you have travelled. For a canoeist with limited equipment it is difficult to know the exact paddling speed with the tide and similarly steering on a compass course also seems less exact. However, practising both of these in times when you are not dependent on them, will increase your ability to make judgements with a greater degree of accuracy. Using a watch and timing distances in varying conditions will also give you some idea of how fast you can travel. This information will be needed for planning trips, to calculate in advance the distances you will want to travel in fixed amounts of time.

The six minute rule

This is an easy rule to remember. Use it to work out your speed or your distance. (6 minutes is $\frac{1}{10}$th of an hour.)

Travelling for 6 minutes at 2 knots you will do 0.2 nautical miles.

Travelling for 6 minutes at 3 knots you will do 0.3 nautical miles.

Travel 0.5 nautical miles in 6 minutes and you will be travelling at 5 nautical knots.

Travel 2.87 nautical miles in 6 minutes and you will be travelling at 28.7 knots.

Nautical miles and knots

A nautical mile is a unit of length at sea which is one minute of latitude at a given position. It is a little further than a mile on the road. The international nautical mile is 1852m (6076.12ft) on which the speed at sea is based and is called knots. One knot is one nautical mile per hour and equals 1.852 km/h or 0.5144 m/sec or 1.15 mph.

To measure a nautical mile on a chart, go to the side of the chart to the lines of latitude which run from west to east opposite to where you want to measure. The latitude scale is marked in degrees and minutes. For example, on the diagram on page 168 the numbers at the side of the diagram refer to degrees and minutes of latitude.

The effect of the tide

You know how fast you can paddle and in which direction you want to travel so now you need to work out how fast the tide is moving and in what direction. If you paddle at a speed of 3 knots and you want to get to a point 9 nautical miles away with no tide and wind, then it will take you 3 hours. If the tide is going with you in the same direction at a speed of 1 knot, then the distance will take you 2 hours and 20 minutes. If the tide is against you, then you will take 4 hours and 30 minutes. If the tide is moving from left to right, then you would end up about 3 nautical miles to the right of your intended target unless you angled your boat and did a large ferry glide or changed your starting point and took advantage of the tide.

Finding tidal height, rate and direction

The height and times of high water (H.W.) and low water (L.W.) can be found in tide tables, either in a nautical almanac or in small local tide-tables printed for specific areas. From the height you can work out the spring and neap range.

The tidal stream atlas will give you hourly rates and direction for both spring and neap tides, relative to high water of a specific place or Standard Port such as Dover. Look up the time of high water at Dover or the nearest Standard Port to you and find the difference in the time of high water between the port and where you are. For example, I am at Aberdovey and the time of high water at Aberdovey occurs 3 hours 20 minutes before high water at Dover. The Standard Port for Aberdovey is Milford Haven and high water occurs at Aberdovey 2 hours 15 minutes after high water at Milford Haven. Nautical almanacs will refer to the time and height differences relative to the Standard Ports. Once you have the time difference write these times on the appropriate pages of the tidal stream atlas in pencil starting with the high water times. Now you have the direction and rate of the tide for each hour before and after high water. Do not forget that the tide tables are usually calculated on Greenwich Mean Time (GMT), so remember to add the hour, if you need to, for British Summer Time (BST).

To find the direction and rate of the tide from a chart, look for the purple or black tidal diamonds with a letter inside in the area where you need the information. Then read the direction and rates of flow in the box of information on the chart which correlates to the letter inside the tidal diamond. These will give you the hourly direction and rate of flow for spring (Sp) and neap (Np) tides, which also refer to high water at a port such as Dover. If you are between spring and neap tides you have to guess an average rate somewhere between the two for each hour.

Along the coast or sea crossing?

There are two types of trips you can plan. One is along the coast and the other is a sea crossing. Generally the tide runs parallel with the coast, so if you want to head out to an island off the coast, you will probably need to cross the tide. If the island is only a short distance away you should be able to pick the slackest time of the tide to travel quite easily. If the island is further away, however, then you need to do more complex calculations such as tidal vectors, but then you are doing a much more advanced sea trip and that is not covered here.

Timing your trip with the tide

By consulting the tidal diamond information overleaf (or tidal stream atlas), we can see that there is slack water at high water, and for the first hours before and after high water, the tide moves in opposite directions and at the same rate. (A total of three hours' time).

		A 50° 42' 5N 0° 40' 2E		
		Dir	Rate (kn)	
			Sp	N
Before H.W.	6	280	1.0	0.5
	5	285	1.5	1.0
	4	290	2.0	1.5
	3	290	2.0	1.5
	2	295	1.5	1.0
	1	300	1.0	0.5
H.W.		000	slack	
After H.W.	1	120	1.0	0.5
	2	115	1.5	1.0
	3	110	2.0	1.5
	4	110	2.0	1.5
	5	105	1.5	1.0
	6	100	1.0	0.5

Tidal diamond showing direction and speed of tide flow

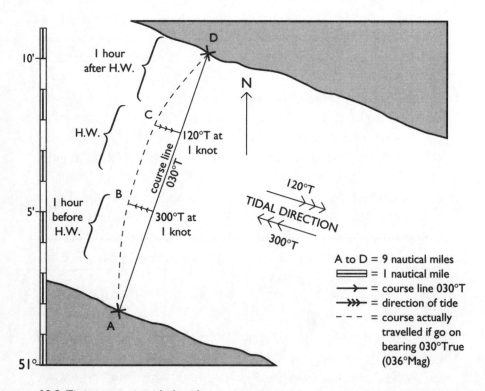

10.3 Timing your trip with the tide.

In figure 10.3 if we were to leave point A and paddle to point D, at the end of the first hour (before high water) we would be at point B, at the end of the second hour, which is slack water, we would be at point C, and at the end of the third hour we would be at point D, our destination. This kind of navigation is easy and does not involve great amounts of chartwork and, as long as the tidal directions are approximately in opposition and with similar rates, this method of navigation for sea paddling is quite acceptable.

Aiming off

If you cannot get enough information on the tidal stream rates and the distance is not very far, then you may have to make an educated guess based on previous paddling experience. You need to aim off towards a point on the uptide side of your destination. This is also a useful technique in windy conditions.

Rules of the 'road'

This is the basis of the law at sea which states who has right of way and during what circumstances (just like traffic on the roads) and it MUST be obeyed by ALL vessels at sea. Unfortunately canoeists are at the bottom of the pecking order in these rules no matter what the conditions or circumstances. Canoes are shallow drafted and easy to manoeuvre and this is generally the basis on which the decision is made on who gives way to who. Even if a vessel does have right of way and it is not being given ALL vessels MUST take avoiding action to prevent a collision. The best way to remember this rule is that if it is bigger than a canoe do not argue with it, especially as canoeists are very small and may not be seen. So keep well clear.

Weather

The only predictable thing about the weather is that it is unpredictable. It is a complex science and impossible to explain with any justice here, but there are many good books on meteorology which cover the subject in great detail. As a responsible and safe sea paddler you need to have a basic awareness of what kinds of things can happen. There are some trends and signs over periods of time which, with experience, can give you indications of 'potential weather' approaching. To find these out I suggest you ask people who know more than you and read and learn by regularly watching the weather and clouds, listen to forecasts and make your own predictions when you see certain cloud types and formations, noting what happens and in what time scale. The more often you do this the more familiarity and understanding you will gain of the weather.

Weather lore

There are lots of traditional phrases and sayings which relate to the weather and your observations of the weather should help you to decide which ones are more reliable than others. A number of them refer to the fact that the weather in the UK generally travels from west to east, others refer to pressure and the barometer and some relate to the effect of different particles in the atmosphere. A few examples are given here.

We only see colours in a ray of sunlight when the ray is bent and split up into colours by a prism or something blocking its path, such as dust particles or water droplets. The saying 'Red sky at night, shepherds' delight; red sky in the morning sailors' warning' is an example of this effect. A red sky at sunset happens in dry air that is full of dust and in Europe it is a sign of a dry day ahead as the weather is moving from west to east. If the sunset is dull or white in colour then that is a sign of water droplets in the atmosphere and the possibility of wet weather approaching. Water droplets are larger than dust particles and greatly reduce the sun's rays so that the sun appears white as it does on a foggy day.

'The evening red and morning grey, are sure signs of a fine day; but the evening grey and morning red, makes the sailor shake his head.' A red sky in the morning is usually due to high frontal cloud being lit up by the sun from below. This would be an indication of bad weather approaching from the west. If the sky was grey in the morning then that would indicate water droplets in the atmosphere to the east and the sign of the passing of bad weather.

'Mackerel sky and mare's tails, make tall ships carry low sails.' Cirrus and cirrocumulus clouds are high clouds which cause the mackerel sky (small, roundish masses) and mare's tails (whispy) appearance of the sky and are early warning signs of rain and wind coming on the warm front of a depression.

Some sayings relate to the rise and fall of the barometer. A slowly falling barometer is a sign of an extended period of bad weather. A quick fall which is followed by a quick rise is a sign of strong winds to follow. 'Long foretold, long last, short notice, soon past; quick rise after low, sure sign of a stronger blow.'

Weather jargon

WIND STRENGTH CHART				
Force	Name used in forecasts	Speed kph/mph	State of sea	Probable wave height m/ft
0	calm	less than 1	like a mirror	0
1		1.5–5/1–3	ripples like scales	0
2	light	6–10/4–6	small wavelets but not breaking	0.1–0.3m/4–12in
3		11–16/7–10	large wavelets, crests begin to break	0.4–1m/1ft 4in–3ft
4	moderate	17–26/11–16	fairly frequent white horses	1–1.5m/3–5ft
5	fresh	27–34/17–21	moderate waves, many white horses	2–2.5m/6.5–8ft
6	strong	35–43/22–27	large waves forming foam crests and some spray	3–4m/10–13ft

Weather forecasts use particular words and phrases which have specific meanings. You should know what these are and be able to interpret them. For example, on the shipping forecast the words 'imminent', 'soon' and 'later' refer to a specific time frame in which things are expected to happen. Imminent means within six hours of issue, soon means six to 12 hours and later means 12 hours or more. It is the same with visibility. 'Fog' means less than 1000m (1100yd) visibility through to 'good' which means more than 8km (5 miles). The speed at which pressure systems move is indicated by the words 'slowly' which means less than 15 knots through to 'very rapidly' which means more than 45 knots.

As wind strength is very important for sea paddlers a scale for rating the wind strength based on the Beaufort Scale is given on page 171.

Weather maps or synoptic charts

The ability to do a simple interpretation of a weather map is certainly very useful as they give information on the position and movement of depressions, including their associated frontal systems and changes in the wind direction and speed. Weather maps can be read a bit like land maps. The isobars on weather maps and contour lines on land maps are both lines which show gradients of pressure and steepness of ground by joining places of the same gradient together. Equal pressure on a weather map and equal height on a land map. The closer together the steeper the gradient, which means the stronger the winds and the steeper the ground. The wind blows almost parallel to the isobars – spiralling outwards away from the centre and moving clockwise in areas of high pressure (called anticyclones) and spiralling inwards, towards the centre in an anticlockwise direction in areas of low pressure or depressions. (These directions are for the northern hemisphere.) As fronts approach, pass over and clear, the formation of certain cloud types and weather patterns is somewhat predictable. Warm fronts usually occur before cold fronts, and as they pass over us, the wind will change direction, often

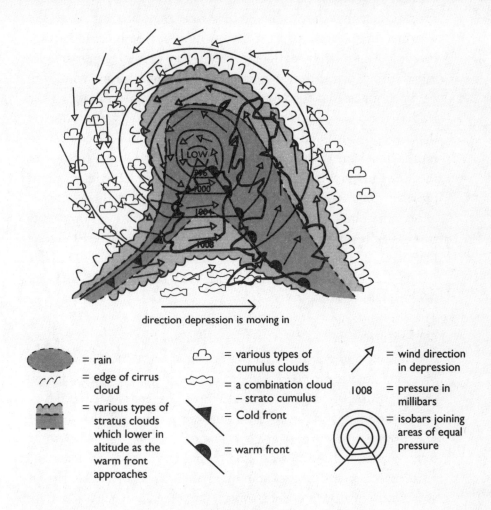

direction depression is moving in

(rain symbol)	= rain	(cumulus symbol)	= various types of cumulus clouds	(wind arrow)	= wind direction in depression
⌒⌒⌒	= edge of cirrus cloud	∿∿	= a combination cloud – strato cumulus	1008	= pressure in millibars
(stratus symbol)	= various types of stratus clouds which lower in altitude as the warm front approaches	(cold front symbol)	= Cold front	(isobars symbol)	= isobars joining areas of equal pressure
		(warm front symbol)	= warm front		

10.4 A depression with its associated fronts and typical cloud formation.

increasing in strength. The heavy rain should decrease and visibility deteriorate with possible fog. As the cold front passes over the wind will again change direction, the heavy rain giving way to clearer weather with visibility improving. Cold fronts are usually more violent than warm fronts with blustery winds and squalls.

Land/sea breezes

There are many small scale local winds that also influence the weather, one of the simplest being the land/sea breeze. The sea breeze occurs during periods of fine weather with light prevailing winds. Calm, sunny mornings on the sea with no wind will rarely stay like that for long. The sun heats up the surface of the land faster than the sea and by late morning the warmer air on the land's surface rises. This rising, warmer air needs to be replaced, which is done by cooler air being drawn in from over the sea. This is what is known as a sea breeze and this cycle of moving air currents around the British Isles creates onshore winds that last until around sunset. During the evening the process is reversed as the land's surface cools down faster than the sea and a land breeze blows offshore to the sea. Onshore winds are a safer direction in which to be blown as they are towards the shore.

Offshore winds

Offshore winds are deceptive because the sea close to the shore gives an illusion of calm, safe water. In these conditions if you venture from the immediate shelter of the coast you could be blown unexpectedly away from the shore, where the wind and waves could get progressively stronger and bigger. On windy days be aware of the effect that hills and cliffs can have deflecting all kinds of weird winds. Sometimes hills and cliffs offer shelter and at other times they conceal downdrafts (winds blown straight down from the top of the cliff or winds that are funnelled between gaps in the land).

Fog

The main thing with fog is not losing members of your group and knowing where you are, with compasses ready to check your direction. It is better to have a compass each just in case you get split up. The fog can cause some disorientation as it is easy to lose the horizon. I remember doing a relatively short crossing in

Scotland when it was foggy and with a good but even ground-swell. About halfway across I became aware that things were not quite the same as they were a short while before. My boat was no longer presenting itself with the same angle to the swell that it had been for the earlier part of the crossing. I was convinced that I had changed direction and it was as much as I could do to stare intensely at my compass expecting it to let me know that I really had. Well I had not. It was the swell that had changed direction but all the same it was disconcerting for a while.

Sun

Bright sunshine, although very pleasant to have around, not only burns unprotected skin but will burn your eyes as well, especially as the reflection and glare off the sea intensifies its strength. Sunglasses with polarized lenses are the most comfortable and relaxing on the eyes. Have a peaked cap or wide brimmed hat available to put on as the sun will be reflected into all parts of your face which has the same effect as the reflected glare on snow. Given a chance it will even burn the underside of your chin, nose and ears.

11

Planning a trip

Trips often emerge from the excitement and spontaneous energy of 'Let's go and do something, something different!' The idea for a trip can be sparked off in a moment but the planning and preparation can take from days to months or years.

There is a wide range of water to choose from and hosts of questions to resolve. Is the trip to be based in one place with different days' canoeing or will you move to new places each day? Do you have transport able to meet you at the end of the day with your equipment, or do you want to carry it in the canoes? Do you want to go somewhere that you have never been before or link some familiar ground together. Do you want to go on an organized event or organize your own? Do you have your own canoes or need to hire them? In what type of boat do you already have experience? How much time do you have? Are you looking for excitement and adventure or to relax and take it easy, or a combination? Are you going with friends of roughly the same ability or the family? Are you all adults or will there be children? Have you ever done a trip before or is this your first? What about other activities. Do you do any hill walking or camping with anyone else?

When I start looking at the number of options that are written here I begin to wonder how on earth I have ever decided what to do for the trips that I have done. I do know however, that the time spent planning and getting everything ready for any trip, no matter how long the trip is for, may be time consuming but it is very necessary and well worth it, especially if the trip is to take place in unfamiliar territory.

The first thing to decide is how long you want to spend on the trip, who you are going with and where to go. Considering the present level of ability of the paddlers is important. How proficient are you all? What are the overall strengths in your skills and what do you lack? What level of first aid do you have? and so on. Trips can be fairly close to civilization where you can easily bail out if there is a problem or give yourselves an opportunity to sort it out, or you can be more wilderness based where you will have to improvize and depend on each other more.

The first trips I did were just day trips, in small groups carrying everything we needed in our boats. The progression from day trips has led quite naturally to one or two days' paddling with overnight bivvies (meagre shelter, if at all) and then trips for several days in more remote places with camping, and then several months at a time, both camping and bivvying in the UK and abroad. Now, when I do any trips I seem to hover somewhere between them all.

It seems only natural therefore, to begin with an overnight trip. There is actually very little difference between an overnight trip and a longer one, the requirements being much the same except for the amount of food which increases proportionally. An overnight trip however, will give you the chance to iron out any problems you may discover on the way which you will probably need to put right before you do a longer trip. These problems may be to do with your equipment or your body. Simple things like sitting in a boat for a longer time than you are used to, how frequently you need to stop to stretch your muscles or tend to your natural bodily functions, how much food and liquid you need, how hot you get when you are paddling and how cold you get when you stop, what combination of clothes is the best for you and where did the snacks all end up (!) all take time and personal experience to work out.

Equipment for overnight
Having decided to go overnight, the equipment you need in addition to your normal paddling gear will be different depending on

whether you are camping or you are staying in bed and breakfast accommodation. There are various interpretations of what the word 'camping' means to people. For some it is the luxury of marquees and deck-chairs and for others, tents usually meant for one person somehow squeezing in three. So I hope to pitch this (excuse the pun) somewhere in between and then you can decide for yourselves.

There is a very fine balance between the amount of equipment that you would like to take and what you can fit into your boat. An open canoe has much more potential for carrying a marquee than does a low-line slalom kayak, so your choice of boat may be determined by what you want to fit into it (that is if you have more than one boat to choose from). Otherwise the only training I can suggest is doing lots of complex three-dimensional jig-saw puzzles or practising the often resorted to technique of self-discipline or going without!

Back to what you REALLY need!

Sleeping

A tent or tents with all the component parts, which will be big enough to accommodate the number of people on the trip. If you do not use it on a regular basis, I suggest putting it up to check that it is complete or at least to find out how many improvized bits you might need to make it work. I hope you do not have mice!

A mattress or something to sleep on such as a basic closed-cell foam mat. Closed-cell foam is different to open-cell foam which is the sponge variety. If you do not understand the difference you will soon find out when the foam gets wet.

A sleeping bag or something to sleep in. If you do not have a sleeping bag that you think will be warm enough then sleep in some warm clothes as well. Sleeping bags are made of many different materials and I suggest using one with a filling made of artificial fibre. Feather or down fillings will not keep you warm when they are wet (or should I have said IF they get wet!).

That is all you need for sleeping. You can improvize most things that you do not have. Pillows can be made out of clothes or bags stuffed with soft items to get the required shape and height.

Food

For cooking you can choose to cook food or take food with you that you can eat cold. People preferring cold food and drink do exist, I have paddled with them! On one trip, a friend did not have a single item of hot food or drink, not even when I offered her one – and I thought I was fairly minimalist. If you decide to cook you need a stove of your choice with the right fuel to go with it and the right amount. Take matches AND a lighter just in case! Of course you will need things with which to cook and eat the food. If you forget your spoon, suitable pieces of wood make good chop sticks and help slow down the process of food consumption. Mug and bowl can be one and the same item or separate ones. A scourer is useful for washing up or you can use gravel, sand or silt.

Food is a huge and varied topic. Basically it should be easy to cook, taste good and be enough for everyone, both in quantity and in calories. It is more feasible to take fresh food on short trips than on longer journeys. Dehydrated food is good if you are short of space, but for an evening meal I would rather take rice, pasta or dried potato powder and add things to that such as vegetables, cheese or fish (depending on your preferred diet). Herbs, spices, seasoning, garlic and packets of soup or stock cubes all help with the flavouring.

Lunch could be sandwiches, soup, cheese, dried fruit and nuts – the choice is fairly wide-ranging and depends on the weather and season. Breakfast could be muesli, porridge, or a full cooked breakfast, again depending on how much you like to eat and wash up and how much time you have. Drinks are personal choice again – tea, coffee, chocolate, soup, water, fruit juice and milk are all options.

Clothing

This is in addition to your paddling clothes and should consist of a complete change, including jumpers with enough insulation to keep you warm for the time of year.

Do not forget footwear and a small towel. Hats and gloves are always useful no matter what the time of year as are your water-proofs. Remember that you probably will not be able to just 'nip inside' out of the rain.

Others

You will probably need a light of some form, battery operated and portable is best. A head torch is a good idea as it leaves your hands free in case you end up carrying your canoes in the dark. Candles are nice and save batteries, but watch out for flammable fabric, especially if you only have one entrance into and out of your tent. Keep a knife handy in case the worst happens and you have to cut yourself out of the tent. This will give you an escape route and a graphic story to relate at a later date!

A minimal wash kit, sharing soap and toothpaste among you saves space. Take reading material and a log book is useful to record helpful data for future trips or anything else which will act as a record of your experience.

Packing

Now you have set aside what you want to take it just has to be waterproofed and put in the canoe!

The trick is to pack in reverse. What you want out first, put in at the end and vice versa. You need to think through the day logically, because if you want a hot drink at lunch time and you do not have a vacuum flask, then all parts of the stove and pots need to be accessible.

The order in which you pack things is important not only for safety equipment, but to save time which may be precious and to prevent frustration in having to unpack everything to find what you want.

Packing for an open canoe

Rucksacks lined with a couple of good heavy-gauge plastic bags make good containers, or use any rip-proof material to protect the plastic liner.

Only waterproof the equipment that really needs it, such as your sleeping bag, clothes, food and inner tent. I prefer to use a couple of heavy-gauge plastic bags to line each rucksack and put my sleeping bag, clothes and food into separate stuff sacks lined with a thinner, bin liner type bag as well. You can be certain that if there is water in the bottom of the boat and the rucksack is lying in it, then any place where water can seep in and get your kit wet, it will!

Fuel and stove: The fuel and stove need to be kept away from food, utensils, pots and anything else that can be contaminated. I know from personal experience that cheese will absorb strong fumes, especially if you have done recent fibreglass work on your boat and you put the cheese, even well wrapped, into the same enclosed compartment in which the repair was done. The cheese then becomes inedible unless you have the stomach for the taste of fibreglass and resin!

Camera: If you have a camera and want to keep it dry but easily accessible, then an ammunition box lined with some padding, makes an excellent, cheap container.

Make sure you test the seal well before you trust the box with your camera though.

First aid kit: I prefer to keep the first aid kit and survival bag in a separate container so that they are easily accessible. Each item however will need to be waterproofed and the container lined and well sealed.

Repair kit: The repair kit for the boats and bits of string and so on can go into the pocket of a rucksack or somewhere where you know they can be found if needed.

Spare paddles can be stowed loose in the boat. Use a piece of elastic or string as a leash around the handle to tie it to the boat so it will not float away in a capsize.

Using space and boat trim

The type of canoe you have will affect how much equipment you can carry and how easy it will be to make waterproof. In an open canoe I have carried enough food and equipment for three weeks at a time, including two 5 gallon containers of drinking water. The open canoe at this point is however, no longer very open, weighs in at about 450kg (1000lbs) and is not very manoeuvrable! A kayak cannot hope to compete with this because it is so much smaller and you are only likely to get as much inside as you would in a mountain expedition rucksack. Maximizing space is therefore important.

In an open canoe finding enough space is certainly not a problem. When you pack the boat, balance the weight equally from side to side. You will probably need to trim the boat somewhat from bow to stern as it should ride slightly higher in the bow under normal conditions.

Packing a general purpose kayak

The type of buoyancy you have will affect this process immensely. Air bags are definitely better because you can deflate the ones you do not need as your equipment will be waterproof and contain enough air and volume to replace what was in the bags. Solid foam blocks limit space, but removing them can dangerously reduce the strength of the kayak. A bulkhead footrest, however, can be removed to store gear in the gaps behind, then it can be replaced. You are much more limited in a kayak of this size and so careful shape and placement of bags is more important. The contents of a rucksack as described above can be squeezed into a kayak depending on your type of buoyancy and type of footrest. Smaller, sausage-shaped bags will help this process and all the air will need squeezing out of them. Do not try and cram as many things as you can into each bag, leave some room in the bags so that you can slide the contents around to fit into all the spaces which you will definitely need to use.

Pack the smaller, crushable items in first such as clothes, tent,

Heavy

Light

11.1 A loaded kayak. Keep heavy things nearest the cockpit and away from the ends.

flysheet, food for the evening and so on, with your sleeping bag and 'mattress' closer to the cockpit as they will be bulky. You can squeeze some types of mattress into awkward spaces as they will bend, or you can fold them flat right behind the cockpit and put other kit on the top. Slide the tent poles down the outside of the bags, making sure that they are well secured, or you can slide them beside your seat as long as they will not get in your way. It is important not to have anything in the cockpit that you might get tangled with. The rest of the equipment fills the spaces in between and as you will not be on your own you will not have to worry about getting it all in to your kayak anyway.

The open canoe and the general-purpose kayak are the more extreme canoes in terms of space for packing with camping kit. Other canoes will fit somewhere between the two and the principles of packing are the same for all canoes. Weight is kept as close to the centre or cockpit as possible, not forgetting the side to side balance as well.

When you get to the water to start your trip allow yourself plenty of time to do the packing, because it can be fiddly and time consuming trying to get everything that you want to take into the boat. Spare paddles are better inside the boat, but for flat, non-moving water it is all right to attach them to the deck on the outside.

Additional equipment for non-moving water

If you are paddling on lakes, canals or very slow moving rivers then you would need no more than what has already been mentioned. If you only have short painters for the open canoes, then longer pieces of rope may be useful to extend them, for tying up to banks or lining them (see lining below) along canals or the river or to tow each other with if necessary.

Maps of the area are necessary and there may even be a canoeing guide written on the waterway you have chosen.

Additional information for trips on white water

For white water there is more to think about in terms of rescue as loaded boats get pinned very easily on rocks and other obstructions, because they are heavier, lower in the water and far less manoeuvrable. A far better option is to portage and carry the equipment around the rapid to avoid this possibility, unless it is so shallow that you can do a combination of wading (as long as the water is no deeper than to your knees) and, in open canoes, lining. The principle of lining can be adapted to kayaks if you have two pieces of rope about 4–5m (13–16ft) long to tie to the bow and stern and you attach the spray-deck to the kayak making sure that it is tied up at the waist tube.

Lining

Lining is using the painters to guide the boat down sections of white water from the shore and it is a skill which requires practice if you want to keep your boat upright and not get it pinned or swamped. The same skills are required for lining as for ferry gliding and eddy-setting. The difference is that you have to use the painters to either provide momentum or slow the boat down to manoeuvre past obstructions. In the rapids because you cannot edge the boat, it is critical to keep the boat as parallel to the current as possible to prevent it being tipped over, particularly as the painters are generally attached quite high on the boat. Weight the downstream end of the canoe slightly heavier than the upstream end to help prevent pinning on obstructions.

Additional information for trips on the sea

For trips on the sea more safety equipment and knowledge of navigation and weather are all necessary. The basics for other equipment required, tides, navigation, rules of the road and weather are described in Chapter 10 on pages 159-75. More information can also be found further on in this chapter under Sea trip suggestions on page 190.

The journey

Once you are under way on your trip, any pressures involved in the organization just seem to disappear. You can enjoy the here and now feeling that the everyday world for most people seems to lack.

As you travel along, enjoying whatever it is you have come away to do, certain things should be mulled over in your mind to ensure that the trip will continue to go smoothly and be a success. These are integral responsibilities for safety that are part of any trip and ought to be thought about carefully by everyone. They include such things as: staying together, being aware of each other's energy levels, fatigue, cold, hunger, the weather, fitness and motivation. If the stretch of water is new to you are you able to recognize the bolt holes if plans need to change? How well can everybody swim? How much have you practised rescues? How cold is the water? What clothing are people wearing? Are they prepared for a swim? What first aid skills do you have? And finally do not overestimate your abilities. If in doubt, play it safe.

The camp-site

The camp-site may or may not be known by you, but aim to get there with enough light to sort everything out. The choice of site needs to be considered as it could be anything from scrub-land or shingle on the beach, to a well equipped tourist camp-site with all the facilities.

You need to have permission to use the site that you choose. Above the Mean High Water mark on the coast, the land is generally privately owned and ownership laws exist for this area. The site also needs a source of fresh water, to be flat enough to accommodate the tent, to be reasonably sheltered from the weather, to have somewhere to put the boats out of reach of the water (especially if you have chosen a cave, an island, or a rock ledge) and so on. The site should be escapable from if the weather worsens and causes flooding in the river or very high tides with big waves.

The environment and low-impact camping

This is a big and sensitive topic not totally unrelated to access. The canoe is silent, does not cause erosion or pollution, leaves no trace of its passing and neither should we. Some environmental practices accepted in the past are frowned upon today such as burning and burying cans and other forms of waste. The environmental rules change as pollution increases and we realize the effect that we are having on the world. What is good environmental practice in one area may not be in another, which you will discover especially if you venture abroad on your trips into other well travelled yet fragile and highly managed areas of wilderness.

Water

'Help to keep all water clean' is part of the country code. The much asked question is 'Is it safe to drink?' Water is a precious commodity as so much has the potential to be undrinkable. There are several ways to purify water, the most common being boiling, using sterilizing tablets, iodine and various filters.

Whatever the system there will always be a problem for some people – for example those with allergic reactions to products, those who are pregnant, others who have thyroid troubles and so on. You need to decide which method is the most appropriate for you.

Do not put anything in a water supply that you would object to coming out of your tap at home! There are such things as bio-degradable soaps, but they still do not improve drinking water. By all means use them, but use them away (at least 50m/yd) from the source of water. The same with washing up. Do not leave ANY food scraps! Wash up away from the water.

Other waste

Human excrement and toilet paper is not a pleasant sight to encounter. Please bury your waste well away from any water and camping area and carry a good strong trowel with which to do this properly.

Carry out all your rubbish. It is better not to take lots of unnecessary wrappings with you. Re-package food into more suitable containers before leaving home.

If we really do care for our environment and want clean, unpolluted spaces in which to relax and enjoy adventure, we must become more responsible for our actions. We are only visitors here for a relatively short period of time and I am sure that our children would like to find things in at least as good a condition as we did.

Skills required of the sea paddler

Before even thinking of undertaking a sea trip your basic paddling skills must be proficient. These should include being able to keep yourself upright with the low and high recovery strokes, steering a straight course efficiently, being able to perform deep water rescues to enable you to assist another and towing someone else who is tired or unable to paddle. A few more skills that will also need practice are: repairing canoes while still at sea, learning to roll and being able to negotiate launching and landing in waves and surf. Practice them regularly in safe water when you do not need them, so that if you ever do need to use them, you know how.

First sea kayak trips

Your first trips should all be made in good weather, with no wind or very light winds and in calm conditions. The sea should have no swell or breaking waves and little or no tidal influence. The coastline should be easy to make landings on at any point, such as shores with sand or gravel beaches. A good paddler in good conditions, will be able to paddle at about the speed of a normal walking pace 4.8kmph (3 mph). In any worse weather or sea conditions this will be less, so do not be too ambitious. Do short distances first to build up your stamina and remember you never know when you might need it to battle against head winds which at times seem to spring up out of nowhere.

Basic equipment to be carried at sea for a day trip

Assuming that you are not on your own, this is the basic equipment that should be carried for the kind of day trip and conditions described above. Even though the list may seem long, remember that conditions can change quickly and if you need to land because you are wet and cold, or have someone who is hypothermic or ill and needs warming up and your transport is either non-existent or not immediately available, then you may need all of it.

What you should have

Waterproof bags for your equipment, waterproofs, warm clothes, towel and shoes, gloves, warm hat, spare food, hot drink, whistle, sunglasses, sun cream, sun hat, lip protection, basic compasses, tow lines, spare paddles, polyethelyne survival bag, distress flares, first aid kit, simple repair kit – Sylglass or plumber's tape (see Chapter 4) and money.

All the kit should be waterproofed and secured mostly inside the boat, with spare paddles on the deck and the rest in pockets on your buoyancy aid, anorak or in a bum bag. The things I like to keep on my person are: extra food such as some chocolate, small first aid kit, hat and paddle mitts, sunglasses, sun-cream, whistle, knife, compass, survival bag and distress flares. Everything else, except for the spare paddles and map, would go inside the boat.

General purpose kayaks on the sea

There is an ever expanding range of sea kayaks on the market, both doubles and singles, ranging from day boats to the more specialized expedition kayaks. However, many people choose general purpose kayaks on the sea, as for them this type of boat offers a greater range of flexibility for all kinds of paddling – on rivers, in the surf or on a short coastal trip. This type of kayak will be fine to begin with as long as it is adapted and made suitable for the sea.

General purpose kayaks made sea-worthy

The kayak should be strong, leakproof and of a medium to high volume. Fittings that should be fixed, if they are not already are: decklines, toggles, maximum buoyancy, and a strong footrest which will not trap your feet if they go past it. Strong elastic is needed for holding and securing certain safety equipment on the outside of the boat such as a compass, maps or charts, spare paddles and possibly distress flares.

The greatest disadvantage with general purpose kayaks is that in windy weather their good manoeuvrability, so useful in other situations, causes them to broach and slew off course too easily which makes them difficult to keep in a straight line. What will reduce this broaching tendency however, is a detachable skeg which is a small fin projecting down into the water, attached to the stern of the kayak acting like a fixed rudder.

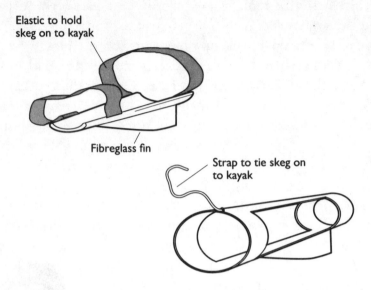

Elastic to hold
skeg on to kayak

Fibreglass fin

Strap to tie skeg on
to kayak

11.2 There are many different types of skeg and it is not difficult to make one for your kayak out of fibreglass.

There are also things that are useful to have like a paddle park, which is a short retainer for your paddle to stop it drifting away when you put it in the water beside you. Other luxuries are such things as a backstrap fitted to the seat for comfort, a sponge to mop out any water and a fishing line. There are many systems that you could choose from when you fit these items on your boat, but in the end asking other sea kayakers what they do, combined with your own experience, is the best way of finding out. Much of this information is personal preference built on other people's knowledge, and experience.

Sea trip suggestions

The information here, needs to be read in conjunction with what is written in Chapter 10 under Sea kayaking.

The season for most sea trips is usually summer, but be wary of the sea temperatures as they are very cold in the spring and at their lowest for the year. A good distance to aim for in a day is about 16km (10 miles) or so, depending on your experience. Are you intending to do a one-way trip or a return?

Once you have decided on what area you want to go to, maps and charts, tide tables and so on need to be obtained, to work out a date when the tides and their direction and rate are compatible with the time that you have available. It may be that you need to go in the reverse direction from the one that you want in order to combine these things.

Once you have a date then more specific information for the planning of the trip needs to take place, such as places to start and finish, to have lunch and other breaks including areas to land in an emergency. The beaches or locations that you choose obviously need to be accessible to you at the stage of tide when you will be there. Another consideration to make is how close you can get your vehicle to the water's edge at any point, particularly at the start and finish, but also at other points along the way if you need to abort the trip for any reason.

Use other people's knowledge of the area too (the local coastguard, other sea paddlers, or fisherman) regarding places of interest such as cliffs or caves and access to them including hazards like tidal races, overfalls or firing ranges. The type of fisherman you choose to ask may affect the information that you get. From lobster fishermen especially, I have obtained some really accurate information and useful advice on local conditions and tidal idiosyncrasies, as they spend a lot of time close inshore in many areas that canoeists frequent. Other fishermen who venture further offshore have on occasions given the most sinister and graphic details of their worst trip out with strong warnings about kayaks not being sea-worthy enough vessels. So accept the information you gain from fishermen with interest and caution, and use it in combination with your own assessment of what you know already about your skill level and what you have gleaned about the possible conditions.

Involve others in the planning and discuss any foreseeable

problems with the levels of ability and fitness, what the weather could do to the conditions in the area and the area's accessibility at all states of the tide. Do not overestimate your abilities. Plan well within what you think you are capable of and be prepared to change your plans at the last minute. Decide how you will come to those decisions before these events happen.

Sort out your equipment a few days beforehand to ensure that you have everything and that it is in good condition. Decide who will carry what safety equipment and so on. Write everything down and leave a copy with someone responsible ashore who will liaise with the coastguard in the event of any concern over your safety. Also give the same information to the coastguard before you leave (see page 37).

Make sure that you have all the tidal information that you need and that it is written on the deck of your kayak or well water-proofed and securely attached to your boat. When it comes to the day of the trip, be ready early as packing is frequently time consuming and there are always last minute things to be done like applying sun cream and any final checks of equipment.

Weather forecast

Watch the weather for several days beforehand to get an idea of what may be building up. Also get an up-to-date forecast before you put out on the water; this can be acquired from various sources.

Forecast sources

- Radio shipping forecast and inshore waters forecast as well as general forecasts.

- Automatic telephone weather services such as Marine Call.

- Facsimile broadcasts.

- Press forecasts – newspapers with synoptic charts are better.

- Television – weather broadcasts showing a synoptic chart are useful.

- The coastguard.

Your sources may give you different information but the forecast needs to be relevant to coastal waters, not offshore or inland. Above all, the speed and direction of the wind has the greatest effect on sea paddling so this is very important information to get. Even if you are a good paddler you may only average about 3 knots (just over 3 miles an hour) and it does not take much wind to stop you in your tracks or make life very uncomfortable. These conditions are the most frustrating for me. There have been times when I have battled mindlessly on, head down into the wind, unaware of the snail's pace that I'd been travelling until I noticed a figure on the shore or cliffs walking much faster than I could hope to paddle. Understanding, at least somewhat, the vagaries of the weather and the limitations that the wind especially imposes on sea paddling are vital.

Useful addresses

Australia
Australian Canoe Federation
PO Box 666
Glebe NSW 2307

Canada
Canadian Canoe Association
1600 Prom James Naismith
  Drive
Gloucester
Ontario KIB 5NA

France
Federation Française De
  Canoe-Kayak
87 Quai De La Marne BP58
94349 Joinville Le Pont

Germany
Deutscher Kanu Verband
Berta Alle 8
Postfach 100315
4100 Duisburg 1

Ireland
Irish Canoe Union
House of Sport
Long Mile Road
Walkinstown
Dublin 12

Italy
Federazione Italiana Conoa
  Kayak
Viale Tiziano 70
00196 Rome

The Netherlands
Nederlandse Kano Bond
Postbus 1160
3800 BD Amersfoort

New Zealand
New Zealand Canoeing
  Association Inc
PO Box 284
6000 Wellington

South Africa
South African Canoe Federation
27 Emmet Crescent
Pietermaritzburg 3201

USA
American Canoe Federation
7432 Alban Station Blvd
Suite B-226 Springfield
Virginia 22150

UK
British Canoe Union
John Dudderidge House
Adbolton Lane
West Bridgford
Nottinghamshire NG2 5AS

Canoe Association of Northern
   Ireland
Clare Medland
114 Upper Lisburn Road
Finaghy
Belfast BT10 0RH

Scottish Canoe Association
Caledonia House
South Gyle
Edinburgh EH12 9DQ

Welsh Canoeing Association
Pen y Bont
Corwen
Clwyd LL21 0EL

Index